ADVERTISING
Paperweights

FIGURAL · GLASS · METAL

MW00388601

PICTORIAL VALUE GUIDE
AND HISTORY

Richard Holiner

Stuart Kammerman

COLLECTOR BOOKS
A Division of Schroeder Publishing Co., Inc.

Dedicated to my good friend Larry Singleton, who introduced me to the Internet.

Contributors: Larry Singleton, Jay Batchelor, Bill Price, Terry Brown, Dot Bowers
Cover design: Beth Summers
Book design: Holly C. Long

Front cover:
    McKinley Iron Works, Cruver, $125.00 – 150.00.
    V. Shoenecker Boot & Shoe Co., $100.00 – 125.00.
    Burr & Co. – Coach Builders, $110.00 – 135.00.
    Newman Brothers, $120.00 – 145.00.
    The Swiss-American Ring Co., $130.00 – 150.00.
    Wells Fargo & Co., 1892, $300.00+.
    Voss Bros. Mfg. Co., $95.00 – 120.00.
    Ort & Co., $250.00+.
    Coates Clipper Mfg. Co., $100.00 – 125.00.
    Sweet, Orr & Co., $95.00 – 120.00.
    Robinson Fire Apparatus Mfg. Co., $135.00 – 160.00.
    The Owens Bottle Machine Co., $300.00+.
    The Electric Storage Battery Co., $130.00 – 150.00.
Back cover, clockwise from top left:
    Sherwin-Williams Company, $200.00 – 250.00.
    New York Edison Co., $325.00 – 375.00.
    The Dayton Caramel Works, $200.00 – 250.00.
    Wolf, Sayer & Heller, $225.00 – 275.00.

The current values in this book should be used only as a guide. They are not intended to set prices, which vary from one section of the country to another. Auction prices as well as dealer prices vary greatly and are affected by condition as well as demand. Neither the authors nor the publisher assumes responsibility for any losses that might be incurred as a result of consulting this guide.

Searching for a publisher?

We are always looking for people knowledgeable within their fields. If you feel that there is a real need for a book on your collectible subject and have a large comprehensive collection, contact Collector Books.

COLLECTOR BOOKS
P.O. Box 3009
Paducah, Kentucky 42002-3009
www.collectorbooks.com

Copyright © 2002 Richard Holiner & Stuart Kammerman

All rights reserved. No part of this book may be reproduced, stored in any retrieval system, or transmitted in any form, or by any means including but not limited to electronic, mechanical, photocopy, recording, or otherwise, without the written consent of the authors and publisher.

Contents

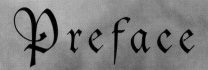

Preface

by Richard Holiner

For the most part, figural advertising paperweights were made for display purposes and to promote a company's product. They were made in various sizes and dimensions and could be placed in areas where flat paperweights could not be seen so well. Figural advertising paperweights became popular in the late 1800s, when businesses began to experience significant expansion and city populations were showing marked growth.

Figural paperweights were made from different kinds of pot metal or iron, even glass, but those of higher quality and more detail were made from better metals such as brass, bronze, and pewter. A common way to manufacture figural advertising paperweights was to miniaturize the actual product and either leave it free-standing or place it on a base printed with an advertising message or a catchy slogan.

The manufacture of figural paperweights was a very competitive business. Paperweight manufacturing companies tried to out-do each other so they could get their products into as many businesses as possible and have their names prominently displayed. Most figural advertising paperweights were made by novelty companies such as Bastian Bros. and Medallis Art of New York, Whitehead & Hoag and the Carwood Co. of New Jersey. In addition, some figural advertising paperweights were made by the companies they advertised, such as iron and steel mills and foundries.

Figural advertising paperweights were designed to depict a variety of subjects. Most were well-made, and many have been around for nearly a century. However, among some considerations to look for when collecting figurals are repairs, cracks, and missing parts. These telltale signs should have a direct correlation to the asking price of this type of advertising paperweight. It is also worth noting that some larger figurals border on being salesman's samples.

Animals were very popular subjects for figural advertising paperweights, especially if there was a tie-in to the company's name, such as "Badger" Fire Ins., "Bear" Bearing Co., The "Crane" Co., etc. The Parisian Novelty Co. of Chicago was very popular for large, round celluloid advertising mirrors.

Some Advertising Paperweight Facts

- The earliest paperweights I've seen have been at Civil War shows, usually primitive and made of stoneware. These are rare and were used by doctors or dentists of that period. Other very early paperweights were the iron non-advertising ones made in most shapes and usually considered Victorian. Numerous examples are shown in this book.

- I've been told that zinc oxide is one of the substances used to seal the backs of the milk glass appearing paperweights.

- Manufacture of paperweights that have original paperbacks and/or are sealed with some kind of substance began around the turn of the century. Three of the most popular makers were the Cruver Mfg. Co. of Chicago, with their painted photographic process; A.C. Bosselman; and the Pyrophoto Companies of New York, with their distinctive sepia-toned styles.

- Glass paperweights that have been made recently are usually round, scalloped, or octagonal in shape. They have unusually colorful graphics with no addresses, and the backs have a crackle-like back seal. Altered or fabricated paperweights usually have felt or noticeably new backs; the text or graphic might be running off the edges, because that advertising was meant for trade cards, boxes, papers, magazines, etc., not paperweights.

Introduction

A History of American Glass Advertising Paperweights

by Stuart Kammerman

During the last two decades of the nineteenth century and the first two decades of the twentieth century, America was increasingly being transformed from an agrarian based economy to a manufacturing economy. Cities and towns attracted large numbers of people moving from the countryside as well as new immigrants arriving in America with the hope of building a prosperous future. As the demographic nature of the United States changed, the role of advertising was also undergoing a major transformation. The mass market was now becoming more accessible to manufacturers, and the need to promote their products was taking on an increasing importance in the face of enhanced competition.

Most of the advertising materials that appeared during those years were ephemeral, paper-based. Trade cards, paper signs, posters, and other paper-based advertising items were distributed in increasing quantities as printing presses and the art of lithography became more sophisticated and the per-item cost of printed material decreased. Many of the non-paper advertising items that were being produced during this period were intended to be given out to preferred or potential consumers. Some of the items being manufactured included celluloid pocket mirrors, china and crockery pieces, and glass paperweights. They were intended to be used as give-aways with "compliments of" the business or firm that wanted to get its advertising message out to the consumer. Most of the glass advertising paperweights were special ordered from paperweight manufacturing firms and were intended to be used as gifts with a promotional advertising message on the obverse side. Many of the paperweights were likely given away by salesmen or other representatives from the various businesses and firms that utilized this advertising medium.

The first glass advertising paperweights to be used in the United States can be traced back to Pittsburgh, Pennsylvania. Lowell Innes in his book, *Pittsburgh Glass 1797 – 1891: A History and Guide for Collectors,* states that "by the 1870s, only one Pittsburgh factory had seriously tried the market: W.H. Maxwell of Pittsburgh's South Side. A fire did $1,500 in damage to his plant on June 2, 1879, but in September he was advertising a paperweight for official desks with the name of the user encased in the center." William H. Maxwell was a key figure in the history of glass advertising paperweights as a result of his being issued United States Patent No. 263, 931 on September 5, 1882 for his process of manufacturing glass paperweights. This patent provided a means by which names, monograms, or designs could be placed on a thin plate of glass in vitrifiable colors. Maxwell's patent of September 5, 1882 described how he would position the advertising message on the thin plate or plaque of glass, place the plate in a mold, and pour clear, molten glass into the mold to cover the graphic on the glass plate. It is the use of this process that gives many of the glass advertising paperweights of the late nineteenth and early twentieth centuries the distinctive white milk glass appearance on the reverse side of the paperweight. Most of the early glass advertising paperweights manufactured by Maxwell were round domed in shape. Maxwell was also issued a second United

States Patent, No. 359, 682, on March 22, 1887, which dealt with his invention of an improved method of forming letters or other characters on glass.

Another early pioneer in the manufacture of glass advertising paperweights was Albert A. Graeser of Pittsburgh, Pennsylvania (between 1891 and 1911, the "h" was dropped from the spelling of the name of that city). Graeser was issued United States Patent No. 487, 013 on November 29, 1892. This patent described another process of manufacturing glass advertising paperweights and specifically dealt with a somewhat different method than Maxwell described of securing designs on glass articles, including paperweights. In reading both patents, one finds there was not a significant difference in the two manufacturing processes as described by Maxwell and Graeser, but there were sufficient variances to enable each person to be issued a patent by the U.S. Patent Office.

Many of the glass advertising paperweights that were produced in the latter two decades of the nineteenth century and through the turn of the next have the name of the paperweight manufacturer printed on the bottom of the obverse side or stamped on the reverse side of the paperweight, showing either the September 5, 1882, or the November 29, 1892, patent date. Early American glass advertising paperweight manufacturers, especially the firms of Brown Maxwell & Co. Limited of Rochester, Pa.; Barnes & Abrams Co. with the locations of either Syracuse. N.Y. or Grapeville, Pa. noted on their paperweights; the Abrams Paper Weight Co. with the spellings on its paperweights of either PIttsburg or Pittsburgh and Monaca, Pa. and which was a successor firm to the Barnes & Abrams Co.; the American P.W. Co. of Pittsburgh, Pa.; the Graeser Mfg. Co. also of Pittsburgh, Pa., all displayed either the 1882 or 1892 patent date on their paperweights. Around the turn of the twentieth century, some glass advertising paperweight manufacturers no longer included either their name or the patent date on the paperweights that they produced.

Flat glass advertising paperweights made by these early manufacturing firms, regardless of their shape, overwhelmingly have the white milk glass appearance on the reverse side. There are very few examples of a green or yellow colored appearance on the reverse side of these firms' paperweights. The piece of thin glass on which the advertising message is presented gives these flat glass paperweights their uniqueness, originality, and permanence. Other glass advertising paperweights manufactured around the turn of the twentieth century had other materials on the reverse side, such as paper, cardboard, mirror, or tin. On round domed paperweights, there is no white milk glass appearance on the reverse side because of an approximately one-half inch thick glass base below the thin glass plaque.

Early glass advertising paperweights were manufactured in a number of different shapes and sizes. The first examples of glass advertising paperweights manufactured beginning in the late 1870s by Maxwell and becoming increasingly popular in the 1880s were small round domed ones, generally measuring approximately 3" in diameter and 1⅞" high. From the 1880s into the second decade of the twentieth century as the art of glass advertising paperweight manufacturing became more sophisticated, glass workers became more expert, and the cost of production continued to decrease, there was a noticeable increase in the variation of shapes. With the passage of time, paperweights evolved, with a rectangular shape ultimately becoming the most popular shape manufactured.

The glass paperweights that were manufactured from the late 1870s into the decade of the 1910s can be grouped into a number of different shapes. Not only was there a variety of shapes but also the sizes within a particular shape often varied in height, width, and thickness depending largely upon the period of construction, the manufacturer, and the size of the molds used. The rectangular-shaped paperweights provide the best example of these differences. Those paperweights that had more rounded corners were the older ones while those with more squared corners were manufactured probably in the first and second decades of the twentieth century.

Until about 1917, all the firms that manufactured paperweights that had the advertising message on the white plaque utilized the patents of September 5, 1882, even though different shapes of paperweights were manufactured during these years.

As indicated in Maxwell's 1882 patent and Graeser's 1892 patent, paperweights could be manufactured in a variety of vitrifiable colors. During the nearly four decades when these glass objects were popular as an advertising vehicle, the overwhelming majority were of two colors, usually with black writing or a black graphic on a white plaque. This is true of all paperweights produced by the Barnes & Abrams Co. and the Abrams Paper Weight Co. Other two-color combinations were:

black & gray	black & yellow	brown & white
gold & white	blue & white	red & white

Three-color paperweights were manufactured in the following colors:

black, white & red	black, white & green
black, white & orange	black, white & bronze
black, white & brown	black, white & yellow
black, green & orange	black, gray & yellow
blue, white & red	blue, white & orange

In addition to the two- and three-color combination paperweights, there are also limited examples where four-color, five-color, and six-color combinations were manufactured. The black and white combination was the one most frequently utilized with the black, white, and red combination being a distant second. All other color combinations were manufactured in very limited numbers. The various color combinations were developed with the passage of time and the increasing technical sophistication of the industry. The same can be said about hand lettering and hand design. With improvements in the transfer process, more elaborate photographs and designs were incorporated onto the faces of the paperweights.

Most of the early paperweight manufacturers were located in the area around Pittsburgh and in the northeastern region of the nation, especially in the states of Pennsylvania and New York. Some of the makers, such as the manufacturing firm of Brown Maxwell & Co. Limited of Rochester, Pa., were in business for a relatively short period of time. This firm, to the best of my knowledge, made only round domed paperweights and was in operation about six months in 1881, out of business by 1882.

By 1917 there were companies producing paperweights in Chicago, Kansas City, Denver, and Los Angeles as well as a number of smaller cities. As paperweights became more popular, the number of manufacturing firms and advertisers grew and their distribution stretched from coast to coast. The states with the highest frequency of use by business advertisers were Connecticut, Massachusetts, New York, and Pennsylvania, mainly around the larger population centers. I am aware of nearly 25 different paperweight manufacturing firms that advertised on paperweights.

The one constant in pricing collectible paperweights is its subjective nature. The bottom line is that it all depends upon whether a collector is prepared to pay the price asked by the seller. To take much of the subjectivity out of the pricing equation, one should use such objective criteria as the quality of the graphics, the condition of the glass, relative scarcity, the shape of the paperweight, the particular subject area, etc. Of the nearly 850 glass advertising paperweights that I currently have in my collection, I have paid from $2.00 to $305.00 for an individual paperweight. What can realistically be said is that the price of antique American glass advertising paperweights continues to rise as more collectors learn about and come to appreciate this early advertising medium.

Most paperweights that are collected today are the traditional fancy decorative art paperweights. Collectors of these paperweights are usually interested in the products of certain glass houses, specific glass artists, or unique art scenes. Souvenir paperweight collectors look for everything from scenes of Niagara Falls to church buildings. Those who collect paperweights showing the faces of prominent personalities may specialize in actors and actresses or political candidates. People who collect commemorative paperweights may concentrate on paperweights showing the various buildings at the Columbian World's Exposition of 1893 held in Chicago. There are collectors who specialize in personal memorial paperweights which are intended to remember mothers, fathers, and children who have passed away. Then there are collectors like me who specialize in glass advertising paperweights either in the round domed shape or flat shapes with the white milk glass appearance on the reverse side. While limiting my paperweight collecting interests to these types, I have a wide variety of subject areas included in the advertising messages. There are beautiful graphics to be viewed, jobs and trades which have long since disappeared, and words of the English language no longer in common use.

Much beauty, elegance, and historical significance can be observed in early American glass advertising paperweights. They truly provide the collector of these glass gems with a snapshot of and an appreciation for commercial and social life in the United States a century ago.

UNITED STATES PATENT OFFICE.

WILLIAM H. MAXWELL, OF ROCHESTER, PENNSYLVANIA, ASSIGNOR TO BROWN, MAXWELL & COMPANY, (LIMITED,) OF SAME PLACE.

MANUFACTURE OF GLASS PAPER-WEIGHTS.

SPECIFICATION forming part of Letters Patent No. 263,931, dated September 5, 1882.

Application filed June 15, 1882. (Model.)

To all whom it may concern:

Be it known that I, WILLIAM H. MAXWELL, of Rochester, in the county of Beaver and State of Pennsylvania, have invented a new and use-
5 ful Improvement in the Manufacture of Glass Paper-Weights and other Articles from Glass, of which the following is a full, clear, and exact description.

Figure 1 is a perspective view of the mold.
10 Fig. 2 is a perspective view of the ring for surrounding the mold and into which the molten glass is poured. Fig. 3 is a side elevation, partly in section, of the mold, ring, and plate in position. Figs. 4 and 5 are side elevations
15 of the punty carrying the molded glass.

My invention consists in a new process for the manufacture of paper-weights and other articles from glass, and containing names, designs, or pictures in colors.
20 The essential feature consists in the covering of paintings or designs made in vitrifiable colors with molten glass, as hereinafter described and claimed, reference being had to the accompanying drawings, wherein I have
25 illustrated the apparatus used in carrying out the process.

The process is as follows: Upon a thin plate, *a*, of white glass, or glass of any color, and of a circular or other shape, are first painted or
30 printed names, monograms, or designs of any kind, as may be desired, and in vitrifiable colors. This plate is then placed in a mold, A, (shown in Fig. 1 of the drawings,) which mold is made with a concave or flat surface, accord-
35 ing to the form it is desired to give to the painted plate, and the mold and glass plate are then placed in the fire until the glass is sufficiently heated. The ring B (shown in Fig. 2) is then placed over the plate *a* and around
40 the mold, as shown in Fig. 3, and into this ring glass in a molten state is dropped, so that it covers the back and one side of the painted plate. The glass thus molded is then removed and "struck up" on a "punty" or pipe, as illustrated in Fig. 4, and the other side of the
45 painted plate is then covered, either by "casting on" the glass or "gathering it" on in the pot. I then cut down behind the plate with ordinary glass-working tools until it is small enough to be knocked off, as in Fig. 5.
50 By this process I produce an article of handsome appearance.

I do not limit myself to any particular shape, form, or size, nor especially to the manufacture of paper-weights, as door-knobs, curtain-pins,
55 door-plates, and other articles can be made by the same process.

One or both sides of the painted glass plate may be covered with clear glass, as desired.

Having thus described my invention, I claim
60 as new and desire to secure by Letters Patent—

1. Improved process for the manufacture of paper-weights and other articles, which consists in covering vitrified paintings or designs upon glass with molten glass by casting or
65 molding, substantially as described.

2. The hereinbefore-described process for the manufacture of paper-weights and other articles, which consists in first painting or printing a design upon colored glass with vit-
70 rifiable colors, and then covering the same with clear glass by molding or casting, substantially as described.

3. In the manufacture of paper-weights and other articles from glass, the combination of
75 the mold A, for receiving the painted or printed plate of glass, and the ring B, adapted to be placed over the plate *a* of glass, and the mold for casting clear glass thereon, substantially as shown and described.

WILLIAM H. MAXWELL.

Witnesses:
HARTFORD P. BROWN,
GEORGE H. CROSS.

(Model.)

W. H. MAXWELL.
MANUFACTURE OF GLASS PAPER WEIGHTS.

No. 263,931.   Patented Sept. 5, 1882.

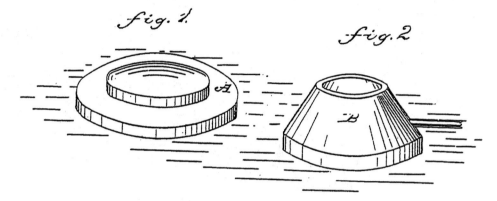

fig. 1.   fig. 2

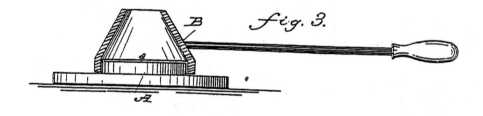

fig. 3.

fig. 4.

fig. 5.

WITNESSES:

INVENTOR:
W. H. Maxwell
BY
ATTORNEYS.

Manufacturers

Paperweight manufacturers who made glass advertising with the white milk glass appearance on the reverse side:

Barnes & Abrams Co., Grapeville, Pa.

Abrams Paper, Pittsburgh, Pa.

Barnes & Abrams Co., Syracuse, N.Y.

J.N. Abrams, Mystic, Conn.

J.N. Abrams, 247 W. 126 St., New York, N.Y.

Abrams Paper Weight Co., Pittsburgh, Pa.

Abrams Paper Weight Co., Monaca, Pa.

Abrams PW Co., Monaca, Pa.

American PW Co., Pittsburgh, Pa.

Samuel Ward Co., Boston, Mass.

Graeser Mfg. Co., Pittsburgh, Pa.

A. Graeser, Pittsburgh, Pa.

The Donker & Williams Co., St. Paul, Minn.

Metropolitan Glass Co., Monaca, Pa.

Met. Glass Co., Monaca

Albert Graeser, Pittsburgh, Pa.

S.H. Soule, Los Angeles, Calif.

Kyle Adv. Co., Louisville, Ky.

The Donker & Williams Co., Chicago, Ill.

E.N. Smock & Co., Chicago, Ill.

Brown & Chesney Co., Kansas City, Mo.

Jeff D. Nathan, Memphis, Tenn.

H.D. Hardenburg & Co., New York, N.Y.

McKee & Slack, Denver, Colo.

Mid-West Ad. Co., Kansas City, Mo.

A	B	
C	D	E
		F
G	H	

All milk glass appearance.

A   Wilson Snyder Mfg. Co., $100.00 – 125.00.
B   Watertown Steam Engine Co., $110.00 – 135.00.
C   Utica Gas Fixture Co., $110.00 – 135.00.
D   Star Oil Company, $90.00 – 115.00.
E   The Laidlaw-Dunn-Gordon Co., $110.00 – 135.00.
F   The Plume & Atwood Mfg. Co., $100.00 – 125.00.
G   Dexter Portland Cement Co., $45.00 – 60.00.
H   The V Shape Wall Tie, $75.00 – 90.00.

A	B
C D	E
	F
G	H

All milk glass appearance.
A   James Williamson & Co., $120.00 – 145.00.
B   Bommer Spring Hinges, $100.00 – 125.00.
C   Metzger & Co. Roofers Mfg. & Dealers, $140.00 – 165.00.
D   General Supply Co., $65.00 – 80.00.
E   The Hendrick Mfg. Co., $70.00 – 85.00.
F   S.P. Shotter & Co. – Brewers Pitch, $130.00 – 155.00.
G   Brown-Lipe Gear Co., $120.00 – 145.00.
H   Warwick Cycle Mfg. Co., $110.00 – 135.00.

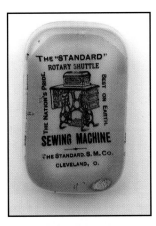

A	B
C	D
	E
	F
G	H

All milk glass appearance.
A   White Star Line, $120.00 – 145.00.
B   Fish Bros. Wagon Co., $115.00 – 140.00.
C   Isaac A. Sheppard & Co., $110.00 – 135.00.
D   Horace B. Walker Mfg. & Co., $110.00 – 135.00.
E   Wilton & Brussels Carpet Co., $75.00 – 90.00.
F   Aiken & Co., $85.00 – 100.00.
G   Champion Steel Range Co., $110.00 – 135.00.
H   The Standard S.M. Co., $110.00 – 135.00.

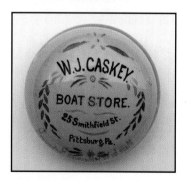

A	B
C	D
E	F
G	H

All milk glass appearance.

A Haines, Jones & Cadbury Co., $110.00 – 135.00.
B Burlington Blinds Best Made, $90.00 – 115.00.
C Morand Cushion Wheels, $80.00 – 100.00.
D Lobdell Car Wheel Co., $120.00 – 145.00.
E American Motor Transfer, $75.00 – 95.00.
F Walker-Lewis Carriage Co., $100.00 – 125.00.
G W.J. Caskey Boat Store, $140.00 – 165.00.
H Great Rock Island Route, $75.00 – 95.00.

All milk glass appearance.

A	B	C
D	E	F
G	H	

A   Weis & Oppenheimer, $110.00 – 135.00.
B   The American Writing Machine Co., $110.00 – 135.00.
C   The Gamewell Co., $120.00 – 145.00.
D   Bixby's Satinola, $100.00 – 125.00.
E   L.W. McArthur Jeweler, $115.00 – 140.00.
F   William H. Lent & Co., $75.00 – 90.00.
G   H.A. Groen & Bro., $90.00 – 115.00.
H   Kurzrok Bros. Co., $85.00 – 105.00.

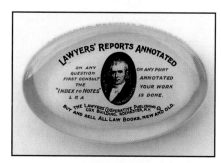

A	B
C D	E
	F
G	H

All milk glass appearance.
A   Brookville Glove Co., $25.00 – 40.00.
B   John M. Burnet's Sons, $70.00 – 85.00.
C   L.C. Childs & Son, $110.00 – 135.00.
D   The Merchants' Index, $65.00 – 80.00.
E   The Lawyers' Cooperative Publishing Co., $70.00 – 85.00.
F   Sam'l W. Goodman 1865 – 1900, $65.00 – 80.00.
G   Teachenor-Bartberger Engraving Co., $70.00 – 85.00.
H   Aikin, Lambert & Co., $135.00 – 160.00.

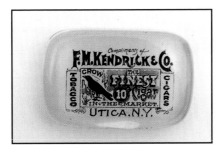

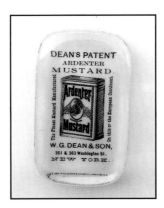

A	B	C
	D	E	
F	G	H

All milk glass appearance.
A   Boston Bureau of Advertising, $100.00 – 125.00.
B   Harry Jarrett, $60.00 – 75.00.
C   Mason's Concentrated Food Co., $155.00 – 180.00.
D   F.M. Kendrick & Co., $110.00 – 135.00.
E   Hunter & Trimm Co., $110.00 – 135.00.
F   Merrell & Soule, $135.00 – 160.00.
G   W.G. Dean & Son – Tin Box, $110.00 – 135.00.
H   Sharp & Perkins, $110.00 – 135.00.

A	B	C
	D	
E		F
G		H

All milk glass appearance.

A   Wm. Lanahan & Son, $80.00 – 95.00.
B   Daniel Frank & Co., $115.00 – 140.00.
C   First National Bank – Ohio, $100.00 – 125.00.
D   The Eighth National Bank of Philadelphia, $75.00 – 90.00.
E   Connecticut Fire Insurance Co., $90.00 – 120.00.
F   A.S. Caywood – Real Estate and Insurance, $65.00 – 80.00.
G   Vanderslice-Lynds Company, $65.00 –80.00.
H   Frank Blacklock, $80.00 – 95.00.

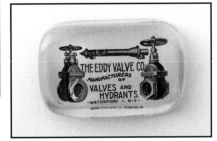

A	B
C	D E
G	H F

All milk glass appearance.

A   McPhail – Gold Medal, $60.00 – 85.00.
B   R.G. Dun & Co., $90.00 – 110.00.
C   Dowagiac Drills, $110.00 –130.00.
D   Kreiter Gear & Machine Co., $65.00 – 80.00.
E   Mahoney R.R. Ditching Machine Co., $110.00 – 130.00.
F   The Eddy Valve Co., $110.00 – 135.00.
G   Cleveland Machine Works, $110.00 – 135.00.
H   S.P. Shotter & Co. – Tar Pitch, $130.00 – 150.00.

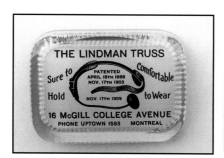

A	B	C
	D	E
F	G	H

All milk glass appearance.
A   Safety Fund National Bank, $90.00 – 115.00.
B   Frank P. Milburn – Architect, $90.00 – 110.00.
C   Klauder-Weldon Dyeing Machine Co., $110.00 –135.00.
D   Louis F. Liotard – Reeds & Harness , $70.00 – 85.00.
E   Ideal Couch & Casket Co., $150.00 – 175.00.
F   The Lindman Truss, $95.00 – 120.00.
G   The Upjohn Pill & Granule Co., $110.00 – 135.00.
H   J.L. Hopkins & Co., $75.00 –90.00.

All milk glass appearance.
A   John Heckel Mfg., $85.00 – 110.00.
B   Duparquet, Huot & Moneuse Co., $110.00 – 135.00.
C   The American Fire Ins. Co., $100.00 – 125.00.
D   Nicholas Burke Co., $70.00 – 85.00.
E   The Peckham Truck Co., $100.00 – 125.00.
F   Chas. Emmerick & Co., $90.00 – 115.00.
G   Chapman Valve Mfg. Co., $110.00 – 135.00.
H   Acme Oil Co. – Penn. & New York, $80.00 – 105.00.

All milk glass appearance.

A   P.K. Wilson & Son, $65.00 – 80.00.
B   The Prudential Ins. Co. of America, $100.00 – 125.00.
C   Macbeth-Evans Glass Co., $60.00 – 80.00.
D   Jos. Fleming & Son, $120.00 – 145.00.
E   Follmer, Clogg & Co., $95.00 – 115.00.
F   Dean & Graves – Arden Heater, $110.00 – 135.00.
G   Isaac A. Sheppard & Co. – Ranges, $110.00 – 135.00.
H   Brown & Patterson – Piano Plates, $110.00 – 135.00.
I   Provident Life & Trust Co., $105.00 – 125.00.

A	B	C
D	E	F
G	H	I

All milk glass appearance.

A   Merrell & Soule – "None Such Mince Meat," $120.00 –145.00.
B   Lamb Club Whiskey, $120.00 – 145.00.
C   White, Warner & Co., $110.00 –130.00.
D   The Born Steel Range Mfg. Co., $110.00 – 135.00.
E   The Sun Vapor Street Light Co., $105.00 – 125.00.
F   Heywood Shoe, $105.00 – 125.00.
G   Alfred Benjamin Co., $95.00 – 115.00.
H   American House Moving Co., Inc., $110.00 – 135.00.
I   J.R. Leeson & Co. – Boston/Haverhill, $110.00 – 135.00.

A	B	C
D	E	F
G	H	I

All milk glass appearance.
A   C.F. Boehringer & Soehne – Red, $60.00 – 80.00.
B   Wetherill & Brother, $85.00 – 105.00.
C   Eddystone Mfg. Co., $95.00 – 115.00.
D   Eastwood Wire Mfg. Co., $80.00 – 95.00.
E   Geo N. Reinhardt & Co. – Gray, $80.00 – 95.00.
F   Magee Furnace Co., $70.00 – 85.00.
G   Allentown Flint Bottle Co., $55.00 – 70.00.
H   The Muhlhauser Co., $100.00 – 120.00.

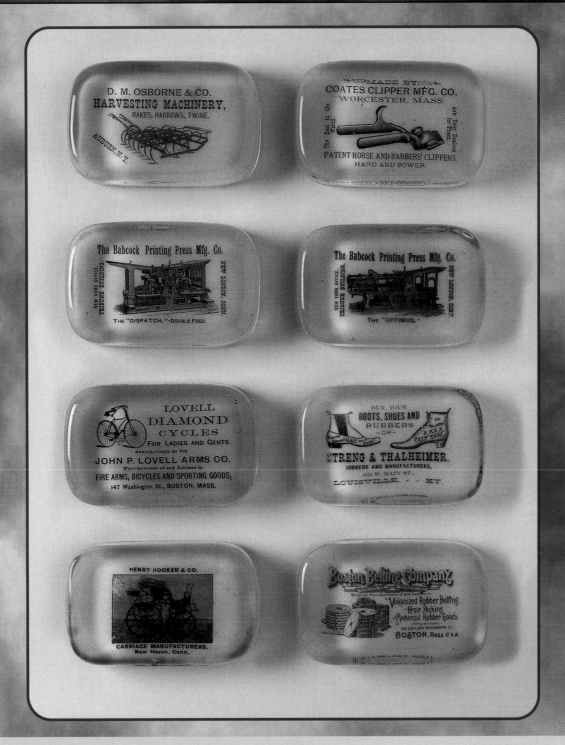

All milk glass appearance.

A   D.M. Osborne & Co., $110.00 – 135.00.
B   Coates Clipper Mfg. Co., $85.00 – 110.00.
C   Babcock Printing Press Mfg. Co. – Dispatch, $105.00 – 125.00.
D   Babcock Printing Press Mfg. Co. – Optimus, $110.00 – 130.00.
E   John P. Lovell Arms Co., $120.00 – 145.00.
F   Streng & Thalheimer, $110.00 – 130.00.
G   Henry Hooker & Co., $135.00 – 155.00.
H   Boston Belting Co., $110.00 – 130.00.

A	B
C	D
E	F
G	H

All milk glass appearance.
A   Eagle Brewery, $100.00 – 125.00.
B   Vincennes Egg Case Co., $100.00 – 125.00.
C   Victor Knitting Mill, $105.00 – 125.00.
D   Groton Bridge & Mfg. Co., $110.00 – 130.00.
E   The S.S. White Dental Mfg. Co., $80.00 – 95.00.
F   W.G. Dean & Son – Mustard/Medallions, $110.00 – 130.00.
G   Wm. Lanahan & Son, $85.00 – 105.00.
H   Stuart Bros. Co. – Blank Books, $75.00 – 100.00.

All milk glass appearance.
A   Bruckman Lumber Co., $60.00 – 80.00.
B   William Reid, $60.00 – 75.00.
C   The Crescent Creamery Co., $80.00 –95.00.
D   A.F. Fox Co. Real Estate, $60.00- 75.00.
E   Steel City Electric Co., $60.00 – 75.00.
F   Mr. Bowers, $75.00 – 90.00.
G   The Sinclair Mfg. Co., $85.00 – 105.00.
H   The Missouri State Life Ins. Co., $50.00 – 65.00.
I   The Prudential Ins. Co. of America, $105.00 – 130.00.

All milk glass appearance.

A	B
C	D
E	F
G	H

A   Minnesota Title Ins. & Trust Co., $70.00 –85.00.
B   Fletcher Manufacturing Co., $60.00 – 75.00.
C   The Pacific Guano & Fertilizer Co., $80.00 – 95.00.
D   Twin Brothers Co., $65.00 – 80.00.
E   Robert Griffin Co., $60.00 – 75.00.
F   W. D. Lacy Coal Co., $100.00 – 125.00.
G   Wm. H. Field Co., $60.00 – 75.00.
H   Thomas Potter, Sons & Co., $65.00 – 80.00.

All milk glass appearance.

A	B
C	D
E	F
G	H

A   Peerless Rubber Mfg. Co. – Large Hose, $100.00 – 125.00.
B   Donaldson Iron Co., $105.00 – 130.00.
C   American Machine Co. Ltd., $90.00 – 115.00.
D   R.S. McCague, $80.00 – 95.00.
E   Norvell-Shapleigh Hwd. Co., $75.00 – 90.00.
F   James Hanley Brewing Co., $105.00 – 130.00.
G   Shannon Spring Bed Mfg. Co., $85.00 – 100.00.
H   McElroy-Shannon Spring Bed Mfg. Co., $85.00 –100.00.

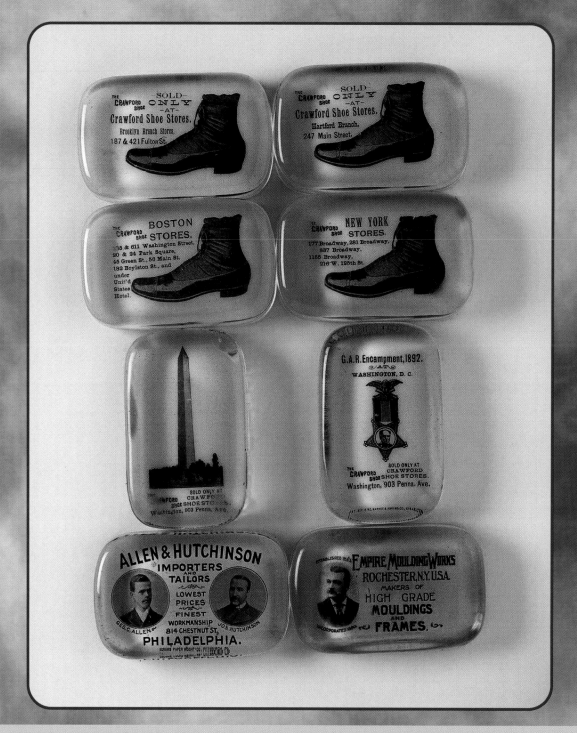

All milk glass appearance.

A	B
C	D
E	F
G	H

A   The Crawford Shoe – Brooklyn, $110.00 – 135.00.
B   The Crawford Shoe – Hartford, $110.00 – 135.00.
C   The Crawford Shoe – Boston, $110.00 – 135.00.
D   The Crawford Shoe – New York, $110.00 – 135.00.
E   The Crawford Shoe – Wash. Monu., $100.00 – 125.00.
F   The Crawford Shoe – G.A.R. Encampment, $100.00 – 125.00.
G   Allen & Hutchinson, $90.00 – 115.00.
H   Empire Moulding Works, $90.00 – 115.00.

All milk glass appearance.
A   Mound Coffin Co., $130.00 – 155.00.
B   Chautauqua Lake Ice Co., $120.00 – 145.00.
C   Acme Lumber Co., $100.00 – 125.00.
D   Cambria Title, Savings & Trust Co., $60.00 – 80.00.
E   The New Mathewson – Hotel & Pier, $105.00 –130.00.
F   Ohio Sash & Door Co. – Orange, $70.00 – 85.00.
G   Sun Flame, $60.00 – 75.00.
H   Ward's Vitovim Bread, $50.00 – 65.00.

A	B
C	D
E	F
G	H

All milk glass appearance.

A Col. Albert A. Pope – young, $55.00 – 70.00.
B Col. Albert A. Pope – middle age, $55.00 –70.00.
C Col. Albert A. Pope – old, $55.00 – 70.00.
D Whitcomb Envelope Co., $65.00 – 80.00.
E Van Vleet – Mansfield Drug Co., $55.00 – 70.00.
F P.P. Van Vleet, President, $65.00 –80.00.
G Allen – Wadley Lumber Co., $70.00 – 85.00.
H Stevenson Co. Ltd. – Doors, $110.00 – 130.00.
I Hotel Review – Editor, $70.00 – 85.00.

A	B	C
D	E	F
G	H	I

All milk glass appearance.
A   The Owens Bottle Machine Co. (side view – 1917), $300.00+.
B   The Owens Bottle Machine Co. (front view), $300.00+.
C   Coates Clipper Mfg. Co. (red), $100.00 – 125.00.
D   The Swiss-American Ring Co., $130.00 – 150.00.
E   The Electric Storage Battery Co., $130.00 – 150.00.
F   Burr & Co. – Coach Builders, $110.00 – 135.00.
G   V. Shoenecker Boot & Shoe Co., $100.00 – 125.00.

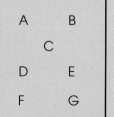

A   Shackamaxon Worsted Co., ground pontil, $105.00 – 125.00.
B   J.R. Keim & Co. – Shackamaxon, ground pontil, $125.00 – 145.00.
C   W. M. Coney & Co., ground pontil, $110.00 – 135.00.
D   Wells Fargo & Co., recessed rough pontil, $300.00+.
E   Standard Oil Co. – Employee 1908, ground pontil, $225.00 – 275.00.
F   Ort & Co., ground pontil, $250.00+.
G   Newman Brothers, ground pontil, $120.00 – 145.00.

A	B	C
D		E
F	G	H

A   S.P. Shotter – Oils, ground pontil, $130.00 – 150.00.
B   Lucas Paint, milk glass appearance, $95.00 – 115.00.
C   The American Fire Ins. Co., polished pontil, $125.00 – 150.00.
D   Chicago City Bank, rough pontil, $95.00 – 120.00.
E   C & WY Railway – M.B. Stantion- Yard Mgr., rough pontil, $235.00 – 285.00.
F   Amazon Ins. Co., polished pontil, $155.00 – 180.00.
G   Jos. Schlitz Brewing Co., polished pontil, $175.00 – 200.00.
H   Collins Varnish Co., polished pontil, $90.00 – 105.00.

All milk glass appearance.
A   Boston Safe Deposit & Trust Co., $70.00 – 85.00.
B   Cyrus T. Clark Co., $75.00 – 90.00.
C   F.G. Hartwell Co., $110.00 – 130.00.
D   The Sam'l Winslow Skate Mfg. Co., $110.00 – 135.00.
E   E.P. Stacy & Sons, $90.00 – 115.00.
F   Champlain Silk Mills, $100.00 – 125.00.
G   Timken Roller Bearing Co., $110.00 – 130.00.
H   The Kan't Slip Shoe, $110.00 – 130.00.

All milk glass appearance.

A   The Louisiana Bag Corp., $85.00 – 100.00.
B   Herrlinger & Co., $70.00 – 85.00.
C   McLain Bros. Co., $90.00 – 110.00.
D   Standard Car Construction Co. – Blue, $90.00 – 110.00.
E   National Blow Pipe & Mfg. Co., $95.00 – 115.00.
F   Wm. L. Elder & Bowman Elder Real Estate, $50.00 – 65.00.
G   Burnaby Brothers Lumber Co, $85.00 – 105.00.
H   Hartshorn's – Shade Rollers, $95.00 –115.00.

All milk glass appearance.

A	B
C	D
E	F
G	H

A   J.R. Leeson & Co. – Boston/Chicago, $110.00 – 135.00.
B   Kale – Lawing Co., $80.00 – 95.00.
C   Dairymens Supply Co., $95.00 – 115.00.
D   Lesher, Whitman & Co., $90.00 – 110.00.
E   Adams Taylor & Co., $110.00 – 135.00.
F   James D. Mason & Co. – Five O'Clock Tea Biscuit, $110.00 – 135.00.
G   Kimball Lumber Mfg. Co., thick, $105.00 – 125.00.
H   John A. Griffith & Co. – thick version, $95.00 – 115.00.

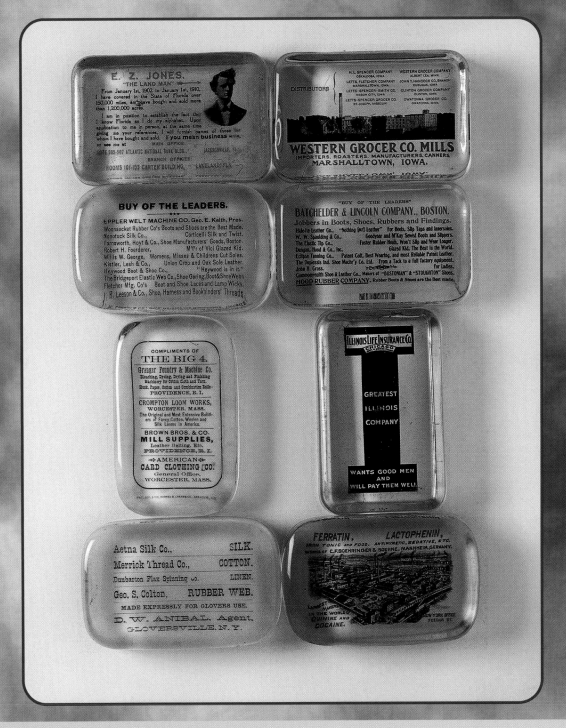

All milk glass appearance.

A	B
C	D
E	F
G	H

A E.Z. Jones – The Land Man, $65.00 –80.00.
B Western Grocer Co. Mills, $60.00 – 75.00.
C Buy of the Leaders – Eppler Welt Machine, etc., $75.00 – 90.00.
D Batchelder & Lincoln Co., Hood Rubber, etc., $75.00 – 90.00.
E The Big 4 – Foundry-Loomworks, etc., $75.00 – 90.00.
F Illinois Life Ins. Co., $60.00 – 75.00.
G D.W. Anibal, Agent for Glovers, four companies listed, $75.00 – 90.00.
H C.F. Boehringer & Soehne – White, $75.00 – 90.00.

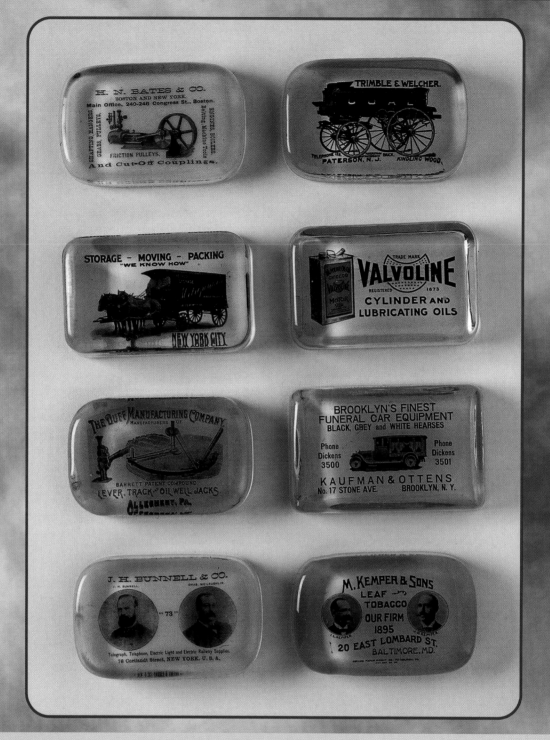

All milk glass appearance.

A	B
C	D
E	F
G	H

A   H.N. Bates & Co., $110.00 – 135.00.
B   Trimble & Welcher, $125.00 – 150.00.
C   Metropolitan Storage Warehouse, $110.00 – 130.00.
D   Valvoline, $125.00 – 150.00.
E   The Duff Manf. Co., $105.00 – 125.00.
F   Kaufman & Ottens – Funeral Car Equip., $110.00 – 135.00.
G   J.H. Bunnell & Co., $110.00 – 130.00.
H   M. Kemper & Sons, $110.00 – 130.00.

All milk glass appearance.
A   Ohio Sash & Door Co. – Black & White, $60.00 – 75.00.
B   Acme Oil Co. – New York & Penn., $80.00 – 105.00.
C   Union Trust Co., $75.00 – 90.00.
D   Jones Brothers – Granite Works, $85.00 – 100.00.
E   Kress House Moving Co., $80.00 – 100.00.
F   Peerless Rubber Mfg. Co. – Small Hose, $100.00 – 120.00.
G   The Snow Steam Pump Works, $80.00 – 100.00.
H   Haggard & Marcusson Co., $80.00 – 95.00.

A	B
C	D
E	F
G	H

All milk glass appearance.
A   Boat Landing At Chautauqua – Devils Lake, N.D., $45.00 – 60.00.
B   Fort Totten – North Dakota, $20.00 – 35.00.
C   C.S. Pearson – Yours Truly, $50.00 – 65.00.
D   Highlands Lighthouse – Cape Cod, $70.00 – 85.00.
E   Cushing Academy – Alumni Dinner 1916, $55.00 –70.00.
F   G.B.B.A. Ball – Bottles, $60.00 – 75.00.
G   Fort Harrison – Terre Haute Reunion, $60.00 – 75.00.

A	B
C	D	E
F	G

All milk glass appearance.

A   Central Electric Co. – pen & pencil holder, $65.00 – 80.00.
B   Omaha Elevator – pen & pencil holder, $65.00 – 80.00.
C   Fink, Bodenheimer & Co. – Diamonds, $75.00 – 90.00.
D   Houston Waste & Fibre Mills, $65.00 – 80.00.
E   The Rust Engineering Co. – change & ashtray, $75.00 – 90.00.
F   International Seal & Lock Co., $80.00 – 95.00.
G   Pocahontas Fuel Co. – change & ashtray, $110.00 –130.00.

All milk glass appearance.
A   Roosevelt & Fairbanks, $225.00 – 275.00.
B   Roosevelt & Fairbanks, $275.00 – 325.00.
C   Admiral Dewey, $95.00 – 110.00.
D   Parker & Davis, $225.00 – 275.00.
E   Buffalo Bill – picture reversed, $150.00 – 200.00.
F   Pope Pius X, $85.00 – 100.00.
G   McKinley & Roosevelt, $190.00 – 225.00.

A	B	C
	D	E
F	G	H

All milk glass appearance.
A   Hibbard-Mason Co., $75.00 – 90.00.
B   Detroit Emery Wheel Co., $80.00 – 95.00.
C   J.A. Dougherty's Sons, $80.00 – 95.00.
D   Wm. Lanahan & Sons, $85.00 – 100.00.
E   Fletcher Manf. Co., $70.00 – 85.00.
F   Robt. D. Patterson – Stationery Co., $105.00 – 130.00.
G   Atlas Portland Cement Co., $65.00 – 80.00.
H   The National Vapor Stove & Mfg. Co., $100.00 – 125.00.

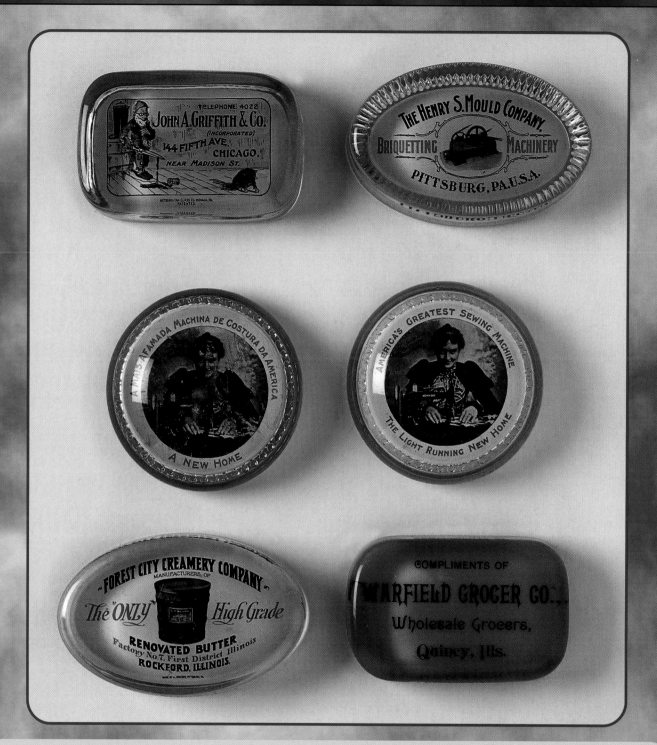

A	B
C	D
E	F

All milk glass appearance.
A   John A. Griffith & Co. – regular version, $95.00 – 115.00.
B   Henry S. Mould Co., $105.00 – 125.00.
C   New Home Sewing Machine – Portuguese, $95.00 – 120.00.
D   New Home Sewing Machine – American, $95.00 – 120.00.
E   Forest City Creamery Co., $80.00 – 95.00.
F   Warfield Grocer Co., $75.00 – 90.00.

A   Acme Mfg. Co., Cruver, $70.00 – 85.00.

B   Bearden Buggy Company, Cruver, $90.00 – 115.00.

C   Chicago Wool Company, Cruver, $75.00 – 90.00.

D   Hackney Wagon Co., Cruver, $150.00 – 175.00.

E   Adrian Knitting Company, Cruver, $70.00 – 85.00.

F   Imperial Valley Stage Co., Cruver, $125.00 – 150.00.

G   Lundin Electric & Machine Co., Cruver, $65.00 – 80.00.

H   Cruver Mfg. Co. Salesman's Sample #66, very rare, $85.00 – 100.00.

All Cruver.
A   Statesville Flour Mills Co., $80.00 – 95.00.
B   Simmons Machine Company, $60.00 – 75.00.
C   Simonds-Shields-Lonsdale Grain Co., $75.00 – 90.00.
D   Western Grain Co., $70.00 – 85.00.
E   Roanoke City Mills, $70.00 – 85.00.
F   Southern Desk Company, $60.00 – 75.00.
G   Lockwood-Hazel Co., $60.00 – 75.00.
H   National Acceptance Co., $25.00 – 40.00.

A	B
C	D
E	F
G	H

All Cruver.

A   Cruver Mfg. Co., $45.00 – 60.00.
B   Hughes-Bozarth-Anderson Co., $150.00 – 175.00.
C   Woburn Machine Company, $80.00 – 95.00.
D   Louis Manheimer & Bros., $80.00 – 95.00.
E   Metropolitan Cab Co., $125.00 – 150.00.
F   Southwest Motor Company, Jordan Autos, made 1916 – 1931, $175.00 – 200.00.
G   Armour Auto Livery, $80.00 – 95.00.
H   Marshall & Harper Motor Ambulance, $125.00 – 150.00.

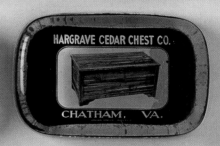

A	B
C	D
E	F
G	H

All Cruver.
A   S. Lando & Co., $80.00 – 95.00.
B   Oklahoma Law Brief Co., $70.00 – 85.00.
C   St. Louis Serum Co., $75.00 – 90.00.
D   Moore & Wyman Elevators, $50.00 – 65.00.
E   F. Horns School of Dancing, $70.00 – 85.00.
F   Hargrave Cedar Chest Co., $60.00 – 75.00.
G   Geo C. Brown & Co., $50.00 – 65.00.
H   Voss Bros. Mfg. Co., $95.00 – 120.00.

A	B
C	D
E	F
G	H

A   A.C. Dutton Lumber Corp., Cruver, $35.00 – 50.00.
B   Doubleday Brothers & Co., Cruver, $40.00 – 55.00.
C   Bates Expanded Steel Truss Co., Cruver, $35.00 – 50.00.
D   Baire Havana Cigars – Cuba, very rare Cruver, $80.00 – 95.00.
E   Sweet, Orr & Co., $95.00 – 120.00.
F   Shedd Aquarium – Chicago, Cruver, $20.00 – 35.00.
G   Union Stockyards – Chicago, Cruver, $30.00 – 45.00.
H   Union Stockyards – Chicago, Cruver, $30.00 – 45.00.

A	B	C
	D	E
F	G	H

A   The Parker Tire & Rubber Co., Cruver, $75.00 – 90.00.
B   Sauers Milling Co. – Infallible, Cruver, $70.00 – 85.00.
C   Logan-Gregg Hardware Co., Cruver, $65.00 – 80.00.
D   Felix Spatola and Sons, Cruver, $65.00 – 80.00.
E   Dent Hardware Co., Cruver, $70.00 – 85.00.
F   Mann's Mortuary, Cruver, $25.00 – 40.00.
G   Western Rope & Mfg. Co., $70.00 – 85.00.
H   Peters Paper Co., $25.00 – 35.00.

A	B
C	D
E	F
G	H

A Pilot Life Insurance Co., Cruver, $40.00 – 55.00.

B Mavar Shrimp & Oyster Company, Cruver, $45.00 – 60.00.

C National Acceptance Co., Cruver, $30.00 – 45.00.

D Central Scientific Company, Cruver, $40.00 – 55.00.

E McKinley Iron Works, Cruver, $125.00 – 150.00.

F Robinson Fire Apparatus Mfg. Co., $135.00 – 160.00.

G O.C. Robuck – Mortuary, $45.00 – 60.00.

H H. Gamse & Bro., $50.00 – 65.00.

A	B
C	D	E
F	G

A   White Star Mfg. Co., $35.00 – 50.00.
B   D.L. Bahn, $25.00 – 40.00.
C   Lawrence Cement Co., $60.00 – 75.00.
D   Gallanis Bros. – Temptation Chocolates, Cruver, $75.00 – 90.00.
E   Maltine Mfg. Co., $60.00 – 75.00.
F   Laidlaw-Dunn-Gordon Co., $70.00 – 85.00.
G   D.S. Walton & Co., $65.00 – 80.00.

A	B
C D	E
F	G

A   M.J. Corliss – Grocer, tinback-3 dice, $105.00 – 130.00.
B   Thomas-Kinzey Lumber Co., tinback-4 dice, $100.00 – 125.00.
C   Lipe Walrath Broom Sewing Machine, tinback-5 dice, $135.00 – 160.00.
D   Forest City Paints, tinback-5 dice, $100.00 – 125.00.
E   Elberon Harness Co., tinback, $110.00 – 135.00.
F   Bartholomew Co., tinback, $115.00 – 140.00.
G   Novelty Skirt & Suit Co., tinback, $50.00 – 65.00.

A	B
C	D
E F	G

A Kreider-Cushman Co., Cruver, $45.00 – 60.00.
B Eastern Maine Steel Ceiling Co., Cruver, $75.00 – 90.00.
C Peter Smith Heater Co., tinback-5 dice, $125.00 – 150.00.
D Cawston Ostrich Farm, tinback-5 dice, $130.00 – 155.00.
E Graham Glass Co., $80.00 – 95.00.
F Geneva, $40.00 – 55.00.
G French Cable Co., $35.00 – 50.00.

A	B
C	D	E
F	G	H

A   Madeira Hill & Co., $20.00 – 35.00.
B   Osmundson – Speed E. Sweeps, $20.00 – 35.00.
C   Atlas Porland Cement Co., $55.00 – 70.00.
D   Skillman, $60.00 – 75.00.
E   Isaac Einhorn, $65.00 – 80.00.
F   Enoch Morgan's Sons – Sapolla Soap, $35.00 – 40.00.
G   Central Electric Co., $40.00 – 55.00.
H   Hepworth Stock Co. – Gladys Sylvani, $40.00 – 65.00.

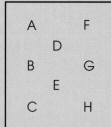

A   C.L. McCarty Insurance, $30.00 – 45.00.
B   J.M. Murdock & Bro. – Lumber, $30.00 – 45.00.
C   Richards & Conover Hardware, $30.00 – 45.00.
D   Pilot Life Insurance, $35.00 – 50.00.
E   Hess Shoes, $60.00 – 75.00.
F   Everett, Aughenbaugh & Co. – Flour, $80.00 – 95.00.
G   Cook's Imperial Wine, $95.00 – 120.00.
H   Grogan's Purity Olive Oil, $45.00 – 60.00.

A	B	C
D	E	F
G	H	

A   William W. Kendrick, $10.00 – 25.00.
B   The Nicholson Co., $15.00 – 30.00.
C   Spatz Wholesale Florists, $20.00 – 35.00.
D   Hampden Glazed Paper & Card Co., leather side band, $15.00 – 30.00.
E   United Piece Dye Works, $30.00 – 45.00.
F   J.L. Prescott & Co. – Stove Polish, $35.00 – 50.00.
G   Shapleigh Hardware Co., $40.00 – 55.00.
H   General Tire Service, $25.00 – 40.00.

All reverse painted.
A   N. Simons – Bitters, $85.00 – 100.00.
B   Wolff American, R.H. Wolff & Co. factory, $90.00 – 115.00.
C   Cudahy's – Pepsin, $80.00 – 95.00.
D   Troy Paint & Color Works, $80.00 – 95.00.
E   American Laundry Machine Co., $65.00 – 80.00.
F   Rock-Rye & Honey, $85.00 – 100.00.
G   Wolff American – Tandem bicycle, $125.00 – 150.00.

A   Fidelity and Deposit Company of Maryland, $65.00 – 80.00.
B   The Liederbach Co., $65.00 – 80.00.
C   G. Sommers & Co., $65.00 – 75.00.
D   F.L. Williamson & Co., $70.00 – 85.00.
E   American Clay Machinery Co., $75.00 – 90.00.
F   New England Mutual Accident Assoc., $70.00 – 85.00.
G   Kaufmann Bros., $95.00 – 120.00.
H   Plansifter Milling Co., $65.00 – 80.00.

A	B
C	D
E	F
G	H

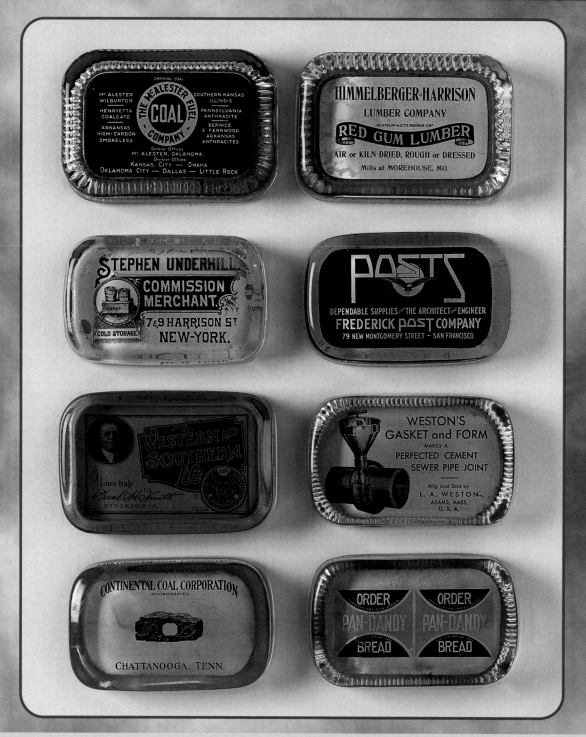

A   McAlester Fuel Company, $60.00 – 75.00.
B   Himmelberger-Harrison Lumber Co., $40.00 – 55.00.
C   Stephen Underhill – Commission Merchant, $70.00 – 85.00.
D   Frederick Post Company, $65.00 – 80.00.
E   Western & Southern Life Ins., $65.00 – 80.00.
F   L.A. Weston – Gaskets, $60.00 – 75.00.
G   Continental Coal Corp., $35.00 – 50.00.
H   Pan-Dandy Bread, $35.00 – 50.00.

A	B
C	D
E	F
G	H

All mirror backed.
A   Premier Distributing Co. – Malt Extract, $60.00 – 75.00.
B   Consumers Coal & Ice Co., $70.00 – 85.00.
C   New Jersey Aluminum Co., $55.00 – 70.00.
D   Mason & Hanson, $45.00 – 60.00.
E   Hudson Cream Flour, $45.00 – 60.00.
F   Rea-Patterson Milling Co. – S and P Flour, $65.00 – 80.00.
G   Keeling Easter Co. – Oyster Shells, $65.00 – 80.00.

All mirror backed.
A   Herman W. Hellman Building, $40.00 – 55.00.
B   Federal Trust Company, $45.00 – 60.00.
C   Peaslee Gaulbert Co., Graeser, $80.00 – 95.00.
D   Pennsylvania Surety Company, $50.00 – 65.00.
E   Great American Ins. Co., $30.00 – 45.00.
F   Henry A. Kries & Son Co., $25.00 – 40.00.
G   Rea-Patterson Milling Co., Sweetheart Flour, $60.00 – 75.00.

All mirror backed.
A   Carl Sholtz Ins., compass, $45.00 – 60.00.
B   Ramsay-Austin Ginners, compass, $45.00 – 60.00.
C   Florida Electric Motor Works, compass, $45.00 – 60.00.
D   Hermitage Electric Supply Corp., dice, $65.00 – 80.00.
E   McDowell & McDowell Contractors, dice, $65.00 – 80.00.
F   F.W. Rickard – Tobacco Seeds, seeds, $70.00 – 85.00.
G   E.K. Hardison Seed Co., tobacco seed, $40.00 – 55.00.
H   E.K. Hardison Seed Co., wheat seed, $40.00 – 55.00.

A	B
C	D
E	F
G	H

All mirror backed.
A   Inland Box Corporation, $45.00 – 60.00.
B   Illinois Pacific Glass Corp., $45.00 – 60.00.
C   Crown Paper Co., $40.00 – 55.00.
D   Stolz Mfg. Co., $50.00 – 65.00.
E   K & K Motor Co. – Studebaker, $60.00 – 75.00.
F   Chas. Seel & Sons, $25.00 – 40.00.
G   Travis Glass Co. – Milk Bottles, $60.00 – 75.00.

All mirror backed.
A   Butler Chain Co., Inc., $45.00 – 60.00.
B   Sprayo-Flake Co., $35.00 – 50.00.
C   Bass Transfer Co., $80.00 – 95.00.
D   Milwaukee-Western Malt Co., $35.00 – 50.00.
E   Alabama Pipe Company, $30.00 – 45.00.
F   Jules Star & Co., $45.00 – 60.00.
G   The Letter Shop, $25.00 – 40.00.
H   Mountain Valley Water Co., $40.00 – 55.00.

A	B
C	D
E	F
G	H

All mirror backed.
A   Dixie Dynamite Distributors, Inc., $15.00 – 30.00.
B   Little Yankee Shoes, $25.00 – 40.00.
C   Sears Tower Chicago – 1930s, $25.00 – 40.00.
D   Tampa Armature Works, $25.00 – 40.00.
E   German American Ins. Co., $30.00 – 45.00.
F   Hummingbird – Jamaican Bauxite, $35.00 – 50.00.
G   Laurens Glass Works. Inc., $35.00 – 50.00.

A   Anchor Fence Co., $20.00 – 35.00.
B   E.C. Poorman Mfr. – Sheridan Troop Cigars, $35.00 – 50.00.
C   Connecticut Fire Ins. Co., $30.00 – 45.00.
D   Buffalo Evening News, $60.00 – 75.00.
E   The McElroy Bros. Co., mirror, $35.00 – 50.00.
F   F. Brody & Sons Co., $25.00 – 40.00.
G   Scribner's Magazine, $15.00 – 30.00.

```
A   C   F
        D
B   E   G
```

A Horse Shoe Lumber Co., $30.00 – 45.00.
B Talbott Bros. – Druggists, $25.00 – 40.00.
C The Rocky Glen Sanatorium, $20.00 – 35.00.
D Frederic H. Burnham Co., $25.00 – 40.00.
E Allen Bros. – Sample Paperweight, $25.00 – 40.00.
F Georgia Dept. of Labor, $5.00 – 10.00.
G I. Gans. Wholesale Notions, milk glass appearance, $60.00 – 75.00.

All pressed.
A   Mander's Varnishes, $45.00 – 60.00.
B   P.H. & F.M. Roots Co., $90.00 – 110.00.
C   Apenta Water, $75.00 – 90.00.
D   Gaylord & Barcley – Tailors, $70.00 – 85.00.
E   T. M. Jones & Co., – Caligraph Typewriter, $70.00 – 85.00.
F   R. Ward & Sons, $60.00 – 75.00.
G   Bell's Asbestos, $80.00 – 95.00.
H   Royal "Ediswan" Lamp, $75.00 – 90.00.

```
A  B  C

  D  E

F  G  H
```

All pressed.
A   Geo K. Hopkins, $30.00 – 45.00.
B   Phillips' Milk of Magnesia, $20.00 – 35.00.
C   The Cambridge Glass Co., $75.00 – 90.00.
D   Smith Corona, $25.00 – 40.00.
E   The Solvay Process Co., $40.00 – 65.00.
F   Morrill Bros. and Co., $40.00 – 65.00.
G   G.A.R. National Encampment 1894, $90.00 – 110.00.

A	B
C	D
E	F G

A   Eddy & Eddy Extracts, etched, $20.00 – 35.00.
B   Star Tailoring Co., etched, $40.00 – 65.00.
C   General John Pershing, pressed, $25.00 – 40.00.
D   Born Steel Range Co., etched, $45.00 – 60.00.
E   Jos. Kuhn & Co., etched, $40.00 – 65.00.
F   Sal Hepatica, etched, $65.00 – 80.00.
G   Jumbo Peanut Butter, embossed, questionable age, $75.00 – 90.00.

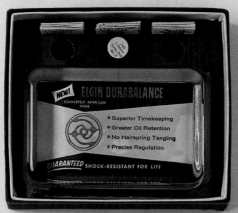

	A	
B		C
D		E
F		G

All paint back sealed.

A   Elgin Durabalance – Watches/both w/parts, $60.00 – 75.00.

B   Winchester Repeating Arms Co., $75.00 – 90.00.

C   Rose Extermination Co., $60.00 –75.00.

D   Siceloff Mfg. Co. – Jeans, $30.00 - $45.00.

E   Orange Crush Bottling Co., $90.00 – 115.00.

F   Ingram Products Co., $35.00 – 50.00.

G   Planters Nut & Chocolate Co., $70.00 – 85.00.

A	B
C	D
E	F

All paint back sealed.
A   The Woodward Co., $25.00 – 35.00.
B   Roden Coal Co., $25.00 – 40.00.
C   Dixie Advertising Co., $20.00 – 35.00.
D   O.B. Kattman Roofing Co., $15.00 – 20.00.
E   Athenaeum Turners, $10.00 – 15.00.
F   Stanley Schultze & Co., $25.00 – 40.00.

A   Ashton & District Mineral Water – Portland, $25.00 – 40.00.
B   Tintic Powders & Supply Co. – Hercules, $125.00 – 150.00.
C   Wm. H. Reinhold, $30.00 – 45.00.
D   W.P. Fuller, change & ashtray, $80.00 –95.00.
E   Telegraph Delivery Service, $25.00 – 40.00.
F   Diesel Engine & Pump Co., $20.00 – 35.00.

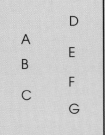

A   Nashville, Tenn. Union Station, $20.00 – 35.00.
B   O.A.K. Jos Store – Idaho, $20.00 – 35.00.
C   Chattanooga, Tenn. Terminal Station, A.C. Bosselman, $20.00 – 35.00.
D   Nelsons 5 Cent Store – New Hampshire, $20.00 – 35.00.
E   Chicago & Northwest R.R. Depot, $20.00 – 35.00.
F   Pennsylvania R.R. Station, N.Y. City, $30.00 – 45.00.
G   St. Louis, Mo. Union Station, $25.00 – 40.00.

A   Belle Isle Park – Detroit, Mich., A.C. Bosselman, $20.00 – 35.00.
B   The Battery Park – Asheville, N.C., $20.0 – 35.00.
C   Ashbury Park – Children's Parade, $20.00 – 35.00.
D   Cedar Point – A. Wehrle, Jr., Ohio, $20.00 – 35.00.
E   Columbia River – Salmon Fishing, A.C. Bosselman, $35.00 – 50.00.
F   Halifax River – Fla., $10.00 – 15.00.
G   Waterfront – Seattle, Wash., $30.00 – 45.00.

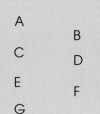

A   Gloucester Fisherman – Mass., $25.00 – 40.00.
B   Soldier & Sailors Monument – Buffalo, N.Y., Pyrophoto Co., $20.00 – 35.00.
C   Oswego River – New York, $20.00 – 35.00.
D   Ausable Chasm – New York, $20.00 – 35.00.
E   Landing Gay Head – "Monohansett," $25.00 – 40.00.
F   Denver Mint & Capitol – Colorado, A.C. Bosselman, $25.00 – 40.00.
G   Inlet Pier – Atlantic City, $20.00 – 35.00.

A   No Monkeying, Pyrophoto Co., $25.00 – 40.00.
B   Longfellow Mansion, A.C. Bosselman, $20.00 – 35.00.
C   Suspension Bridge, Merrimac River – Mass., $20.00 – 35.00.
D   Kennard Bldg. – Destroyed 1902, $20.00 – 35.00.
E   Victorian Lady, $20.00 – 35.00.
F   Chapel – West Virginia Penitentiary, $25.00 – 40.00.
G   Victorian Lady – Actress, A.C. Bosselman, $25.00 – 40.00.

A	B
C	D
E F	G

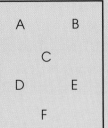

A   W.J. Hardgrove – Tool Dresser, ground pontil, $85.00 – 100.00.

B   McKelvey Co. – Pres. L.B. McKelvey, president misspelled, ground pontil, $60.00 – 75.00.

C   Conners Bros., pontil, $65.00 – 80.00.

D   B & P Lamp Supply Co., Tenn., polished pontil, $55.00 – 70.00.

E   "The Early Bird Catches the Worm," milk glass slab, rare ground pontil, $150.00 – 175.00.

F   Cremens Quality Cleaners – Dr. T.H. Hall, ground pontil, $60.00 – 75.00.

A   HB Instrument Co. – Pres. Frank Hiergesell, polished pontil, $60.00 – 75.00.
B   N.A. Yeager – Attorney, pontil, $35.00 – 50.00.
C   B.P. Lamp – Blanche 1959, polished pontil, $35.00 – 50.00.
D   J.W.J. Shafer 1898, ground pontil, $35.00 – 50.00.
E   W.H. Good – Air Service 1922, pontil, $50.00 – 65.00.
F   "Hard Times in Ireland" – BOB, milk glass slab, ground pontil, $80.00 – 95.00.

A	
B	C
D	
E	F

A   D.A.R., polished pontil, $50.00 – 65.00.
B   Coney Island, ground pontil, $25.00 – 40.00.
C   Atlantic City, pontil, $25.00 – 40.00.
D   Stewart-Grayson – Coals, polished pontil, $75.00 – 90.00.
E   Harpers Ferry, West Va., national monument, polished pontil,
      $45.00 – 60.00.
F   American Can Co., polished pontil, $65.00 – 80.00.

A Admiral Byrd's Polar Ship – City of New York, 1933 Chicago World's Fair, $65.00 – 80.00.
B Chicago World's Fair – 1933 Sky Ride, $60.00 – 75.00.
C Chicago World's Fair – 1933 Federal Bldg., $35.00 – 50.00.
D Chicago World's Fair – 1893 Birds Eye View, milk glass appearance, $85.00 – 100.00.
E Pan American Expo – Pres. McKinley, Temple of Music, $70.00 – 85.00.
F Pan American Expo – Temple of Music, Empire Art Co., $45.00 – 60.00.
G Pan American Expo – Manufacturers Bldg., Pyrophoto Co., $40.00 – 55.00.
H Pan American Expo – 1901, Empire Art Co., $50.00 – 65.00.

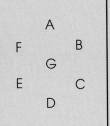

A   Wrigley Bldg. – Chicago, souvenir, $10.00 – 25.00.
B   Nashville, Tenn. – State Capitol, souvenir, $10.00 – 25.00.
C   Museum of Science & Industry – Chicago, souvenir, $10.00 – 25.00.
D   Chicago World's Fair – 1933 Hall of Science, Cruver, $60.00 – 75.00.
E   Chicago World's Fair – 1893 Ferris Wheel, $50.00 – 65.00.
F   Louisiana Purchase Expo – Cascades, $50.00 – 65.00.
G   Art Institute – Chicago, souvenir, $20.00 – 35.00.

All souvenirs.
A Pikes Peak – "Summit House," $10.00 – 25.00.
B Cumberland Falls – Ky., $10.00 – 15.00.
C Cliff House – San Francisco, $10.00 – 25.00.
D Royal Gorge – Colo. – Highest Bridge in the World, $10.00 – 25.00.
E De Ridder, Louisiana, $5.00 – 10.00.
F Corn Palace – Mitchell, South Dakota, $15.00 – 25.00.
G Pikes Peak – "Garden of the Gods," $10.00 – 25.00.
H Broadmoor – Cheyenne Mt., Colorado Springs, $10.00 – 25.00.

All souvenirs.

A   Coney Island – Luna Park – "Helter Skelter," reverse painted mirror back, $70.00 – 85.00.
B   Plymouth Rock – Mass., $20.00 – 35.00.
C   Coney Island – Luna Park, $10.00 – 15.00.
D   The Old Stone Mill – Newport, R.I., $15.00 – 25.00.
E   Coney Island Pavilion of Fun – N.Y., $25.00 – 40.00.
F   Atlantic City – N.J., $15.00 – 25.00.
G   The Shell Fence – St. Petersburg, Fla., $10.00 – 25.00.
H   Grand Canyon – Ariz., $25.00 – 35.00.

A	B
C	D
E	F
G	H

All souvenirs.
A   Yosemite – Redwood – Calif., black bear, $30.00 – 45.00.
B   Yosemite – Redwood – Calif., $25.00 – 40.00.
C   Chandler "Redwood Tree" – Underwood Park – Calif., $15.00 – 30.00.
D   Niagara Falls – Buffalo, N.Y., reverse painted, $20.00 – 35.00.

A   Gen. Mead's Headquarters – Gettysburg Battlefield, Pa., reverse painted, $65.00 – 80.00.
B   Temple Block – Salt Lake City, Utah, change tray, reverse painted, $60.00 – 75.00.
C   Early White House, change tray, reverse painted, $70.00 – 85.00.
D   Early White House, mirror, reverse painted, $45.00 – 60.00.
E   Washington Headquarters – Newburgh, N.Y., reverse painted, $60.00 – 75.00.
F   Early Brooklyn Bridge, change tray, reverse painted, $70.00 – 85.00.

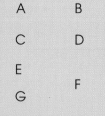

A   Grant's Monument – N.Y., $45.00 – 60.00.
B   Franklin Roosevelt, R. James Farley L., $80.00 – 95.00.
C   Our Assassinated Presidents, $60.00 – 75.00.
D   William J. Bryan, $80.00 – 95.00.
E   Lewis P. Peters – Photographer/Publisher, $35.00 – 50.00.
F   William McKinley, Lewis P. Peters, $40.00 – 55.00.
G   Our Martyred Presidents, $50.00 – 65.00.

A   Flagship Olympia – Admiral Dewey, $30.00 – 45.00.
B   U.S.S. New York – Admiral Sampson, $30.00 – 45.00.
C   Admiral George Dewey, $25.00 – 40.00.
D   U.S.S. Maine, Pyrophoto Co., $60.00 – 75.00.
E   Kaiser Wilhelm II: beveled crystal, white glazed back, reverse painted, $125.00 – 150.00.
F   Remember the Main: misspelled, pontil, $100.00 – 125.00.

A	B
C	D
E	F

A	B
C	D
E	F

A   Steamer, City of Milwaukee, $60.00 – 75.00.
B   Steamer, Mount Hope, A.C. Bosselman, $40.00 – 55.00.
C   Steamer, Washington Irving, $60.00 – 75.00.
D   Steamer, City of Collingwood, $60.00 – 75.00.
E   Steamer, City of Benton Harbor, $60.00 – 75.00.
F   Steamer, City of Benton Harbor, Cruver, $65.00 – 80.00.

A R.M.S. Olympic, recessed top, reverse painted, $125.00 – 150.00.
B Steamer, City of Norfolk, $60.00 – 75.00.
C Steamer, Hendrick Hudson, $60.00 – 75.00.
D Cunard Line, Mauretania: Lusitania, mirror, $75.00 – 90.00.
E R.M.S. Lusitania, reverse painted, $90.00 – 110.00.
F S.S. Finland, $50.00 – 65.00.
G Palace Steamer, Republic, milk glass appearance, $125.00 – 175.00.

A   Bank of Saginaw – Panama Canal, vitrolite, $125.00 – 150.00.
B   Radeker Lumber Co., vitrolite, $100.00 – 125.00.
C   W.K. Kellogg, vitrolite, $150.00 – 185.00.
D   W.K. Kellogg, vitrolite, $150.00 – 185.00.
E   Eureka Glass Works, Inc., vitrolite, $100.00 – 125.00.
F   Hollweg & Reese, china importers, beveled edges, $60.00 – 75.00.

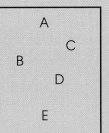

A   Buffalo Co-Op Brewing Co., 1894, pen & card holder,
     $100.00 – 125.00.
B   Heinz's Baked Beans, recessed top, $200.00 – 250.00.
C   E. Hines Lumber Co. – Rand McNally Globe, 1891, revolves,
     $350.00 – 400.00.
D   Holland America Line 1873 – 1948, cloisonne bronze,
     beveled glass, $100.00 – 125.00.
E   Western Cartridge Co., 8¼" x 2¾", $175.00 – 200.00.

A   Cut glass with sulfide frame & picture, 1800s, $250.00 – 300.00.
B   P.N. Mfg. Glass Paperweight & Iron Clamp, 1893, $75.00 – 90.00.
C   Cockle Printing – 1930s: magnifier, print supreme, court briefs, $25.00 – 40.00.
D   Conrad "Rexall" Pharmacy, glass bedpan, $20.00 – 35.00.
E   Fred Waller Photographer, Victorian, $100.00 – 125.00.
F   McDougall – Butler – Stains & Varnishes, magnifier, $25.00 – 40.00.

A   Consolidated Ice Co., $75.00 – 90.00.
B   Obear-Nester Glass Co., $80.00 – 95.00.
C   Cawley, Clark & Co., ground pontil, $30.00 – 45.00.
D   Imperial Color Works, Inc., ground pontil, $60.00 – 75.00.
E   Imperial Colors, ground pontil, $60.00 – 75.00.

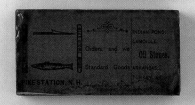

A	B
C	D
E	F
G	H

A   P.J. Sorg Co. – Tobacco, reverse painted, $70.00 – 85.00.

B   Hires Turner Glass Co., beveled, reverse painted, $55.00 – 70.00.

C   The Pike Mfg. Co. – sharpening stone, beveled, $65.00 – 80.00.

D   The Pike Mfg. Co. – sharpening stone, silver plated with cover, $80.00 – 95.00.

E   The Pike Mfg. Co. – sharpening stone, beveled, $65.00 – 80.00.

F   Pike Station – New Hampshire, sharpening stone, $30.00 – 45.00.

G   The Pike Mfg. Co. – sharpening stone, beveled, $65.00 – 80.00.

H   Wm. H. Field Co., reverse printed, $45.00 – 60.00.

A   Badger Plumbing, $25.00 – 40.00.
B   Godey's, $35.00 – 50.00.
C   Cloverline- W.O. Steinmeyer – druggist, magnifier, $60.00 – 75.00.
D   Neill Buick Co., leather, $30.00 – 45.00.
E   Hippodrome Motors – Ford, magnifier, $30.00 – 45.00.
F   Quanah, Acme & Pacific Railway Co., magnifier, $50.00 – 65.00.

A	B
C	D
E	F

A	B
C	D
E	F

A   Heinze's Fine Food Services, leather magnifier, $20.00 – 35.00
B   Campbell & Summerhayes, Cruver, $35.00 – 50.00.
C   Salina Tractor & Thesher Co., leather, original box, $40.00 – 50.00.
D   Campbell & Summerhayes – ashtray, Cruver, $10.00 – 15.00.
E   Weaver's Shoe Shop – ashtray, rubber heel backing, $20.00 – 35.00.
F   Whiting & Davis – mesh paperweight, original box, $25.00 – 40.00.

A	B
C	D
E	F

A   The Garlock Packing Co., composition, $20.00 – 35.00.
B   The Hadden-Rodee Co., $15.00 – 30.00.
C   White & Bagley Co. – Oilzum, leather, $70.00 – 85.00.
D   Central Supply Co. – Oil Field Pipe, $60.00 – 75.00.
E   Buick, 1903 – 1953, $40.00 – 55.00.
F   Knights Templar – 1901, pottery, $50.00 – 65.00.

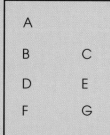

A Viking Lines – 1940 Baseball Series, leather, $25.00 – 40.00
B Woodrow Dawn Wrecker Service – Baseball, leather, $25.00 – 40.00.
C Bush & Gerts Piano, celluloid, $45.00 – 60.00.
D Eastern Milk Producers Coop, pewter center, $15.00 – 30.00.
E Burlington Northern Santa Fe Railway, pressed, $20.00 – 35.00.
F Pfizer-Niamid – Sundial, compass & level, $35.00 – 50.00.
G Maryland Casualty Co., celluloid, $10.00 – 25.00.

A   Dover Castle – England, hand-painted porcelain, $50.00 – 65.00.
B   Victorian Woman, $30.00 – 45.00.
C   German – "Viel Gluck," porcelain beetle on leaf, $35.00 – 50.00.
D   German – Echtes Hans Sitt – Kolophon, $20.00 – 35.00.
E   F.H. Noble & Co. – Chicago – 1930s, metal frame & tin back,
      $10.00 – 15.00.
F   Chief Thompson, $35.00 – 50.00.
G   Victorian Magnifying Star – woman, metal collapsible stand,
      $60.00 – 75.00.

A	B
C	D
E	F

A Steinhardt & Kelly – Fruits, pen & pencil holder, glass, $50.00 – 65.00.
B Victorian, 5¼" dia., brass/iron, non-advertising, $60.00 – 75.00.
C Real Host Gas Ranges, painted metal, $35.00 – 50.00.
D Gorham Silver, seashell, silverplated, $75.00 – 90.00.
E American Emblem Co., 3-footed bronze, silver, $60.00 – 75.00.
F Massachusetts Bay Tercentenary 1630 – 1930, bronze, much information on back side, $75.00 – 90.00.

A The National Safe Co., Cruver, $65.00 – 80.00.
B Detroit Fire & Marine Ins. Co., celluloid, mirror, $45.00 – 60.00.
C Emerson, Smith & Co. Limited, milk glass appearance, $75.00 – 95.00.
D Gillinder & Sons – 1876, Centennial Expo, moving turtle, $200.00 – 250.00.
E Red Lion Table Co., brass, $35.00 – 50.00.
F Philadelphia & Sesqui-tennial – 1926, Aviation Pavilion, Commander Byrd Jr.,
   $30.00 – 45.00.
G Allegheny Transfer & Storage Co., milk glass appearance, $80.00 – 100.00.
H James A. McNally & Sons - Woolens, milk glass appearance, thick, $70.00 – 85.00.

A B C

D E F

G H

A B	
F G C	
E D	

A   Denver & Rio Grande, metal, $20.00 – 35.00.

B   Upper Mississippi Towing Corp.–- Harriet Ann, metal, $30.00 – 45.00.

C   W.D. Wood Co. – sheet iron, milk glass appearance, $65.00 – 80.00.

D   McCurdy Bros. – General Grant, $50.00 – 65.00.

E   Covington & Cincinnati Bridge Co., suspension bridge, paint sealed back, $70.00 – 85.00.

F   Oliver K. Whiting, fox hunting scene, top, roulette wheel reverse, $50.00 – 65.00.

G   Brookville Glove Co., polished pontil, $25.00 – 40.00.

A	B
C	D
E	F
G	H

A   Reed & Barton – Eagle, silverplated, $60.00 – 75.00.
B   Grayson-McLeod Lumber Co., tree stump, painted iron, $120.00 – 145.00.
C   Charles Millar & Son Co., iron, $40.00 – 55.00.
D   Mt. Washington Cog Railway – Dog, Jacob's Ladder, $20.00 – 30.00.
E   Mt. Washington Cog Railway, $20.00 – 30.00.
F   Charles Millar & Son Co., $25.00 – 35.00.
G   Reed & Barton – Factory, $35.00 – 50.00.
H   Grayson-McLeod Lumber Co., milk glass appearance, $60.00 – 75.00.

A   Minnesota Atlantic Transit Co. – Mat Lines 1937, brass, adv. reverse side, $75.00 – 90.00.

B   Military Sales Co. – Memoriam Warren G. Harding, advertising reverse side, $80.00 – 95.00.

C   The Canton Grocery Co. – Ohio Blue Tip Matches, mirror back, $100.00 – 125.00.

D   Rex Flintkote Roofing – grand prize medal World's Fair 1904, St. Louis Button Co., glass, $65.00 – 80.00.

E   Lake Charles Stevedores Inc., mirror back, $35.00 – 50.00.

F   John A. Griffith & Co. – Tailors' Bldg. World's Fair 1904 – Tailors' Trimmings, milk glass appearance, $85.00 – 100.00.

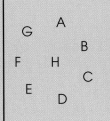

A   C.W. Hull Co. – Coal, reverse has adv., $80.00 – 95.00.
B   Excelsior Wrapper Co., mirror back, $70.00 – 85.00.
C   American Fat Sales Corporation, mirror back, $35.00 – 50.00.
D   Economic Machinery Company, mirror back, $80.00 – 95.00.
E   Mitchell Bros. Taxi – Yellow Cabs, mirror back, $25.00 – 40.00.
F   Illinois Glass Company, mirror back, $65.00 – 70.00.
G   Grand Rapids Cabinet Co., mirror back, $70.00 – 85.00.
H   F. Brody and Sons Co., mirror back, $30.00 – 45.00.

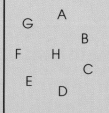

A The Chandler Co., mirror back, $65.00 – 80.00.

B Cyclone Blow Pipe Co., mirror back, $85.00 – 100.00.

C Rohrer & Co., mirror back, $70.00 – 85.00.

D Parisian Novelty Company, mirror back, $50.00 – 65.00.

E Many Blanc & Co. – Shrine Cigars, mirror back, $100.00 – 125.00.

F The Keeley Stove Co., mirror back, $70.00 – 85.00.

G BG Sandwich Shops, mirror back, $30.00 – 45.00.

H Watkins Grain Co., celluloid both sides, $35.00 – 50.00.

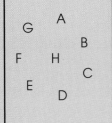

A Lentz – Surgical Instruments, mirror back, $25.00 – 40.00.
B Merchants Motor Freight, mirror back, $35.00 – 50.00.
C Doughnut Corporation of America, mirror back, $70.00 – 85.00.
D S.M.A. Corporation, reverse has adv., $70.00 – 85.00.
E Wilson Funeral Director, mirror back, $50.00 – 65.00.
F Welt and Sons Paper Company, reverse has adv., $40.00 – 55.00.
G Thompson & Jameson, Inc., Elevators – Motors, reverse has 10-year calendar, $45.00 – 60.00.
H R.W. Fitzpatrick – Photography, mirror back, $40.00 – 55.00.

A	B
C	D E
F	G

A   Morton's Iodized Salt, mirror back, $45.00 – 60.00.
B   Griffith Laboratories, mirror back, $45.00 – 60.00.
C   Transo Envelope Co., mirror back, $30.00 – 45.00.
D   Little Rock Blueprint Co. – 1929, reverse calendar, $20.00 – 35.00.
E   The Ohio Overcoat Co., mirror back, $45.00 – 60.00.
F   "The Strange Woman" – Hedy Lamarr – 1946, mirror back, $75.00 – 95.00.
G   Standard Remington Typewriters, mirror back, $65.00 – 80.00.

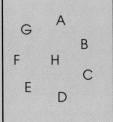

A   Schwerd's – Wood Columns, celluloid/metal band, $60.00 – 75.00.

B   Hornet Mantel Co., reverse 6-year calendar, $60.00 – 75.00.

C   Northwestern Glass Co., $30.00 – 45.00.

D   The Ohio Fire Brick Co., celluloid/metal band, $10.00 – 20.00.

E   Murphy Varnish Co., celluloid/metal band, $45.00 – 60.00.

F   Japs-Olson Printing, celluloid/metal band, $10.00 – 20.00.

G   Turner, Day & Woolworth Handle Co., celluloid/metal band, $45.00 – 60.00.

H   The Steiner Mantel Co., celluloid/metal band, $80.00 – 95.00.

A   Crane & Breed – Toad, $90.00 – 110.00.
B   Crane & Breed – Camel, $60.00 – 75.00.
C   Crane & Breed – Turtle, $90.00 – 110.00.
D   Crane & Breed – Everseal Casket – 1853, bronze, $125.00 – 175.00.
E   Crane & Breed – Fat Face, $25.00 – 40.00.
F   Crane & Breed – Alligator, $80.00 – 95.00.
G   Crane & Breed – Bulldog, $70.00 – 85.00.
H   Crane & Breed – Elephant, $25.00 – 40.00.
I   Crane & Breed – Dog, $30.00 – 45.00.
J   Crane & Breed – Screaming Ghost, $100.00 – 125.00.
K   Crane & Breed – Boojum, $80.00 – 95.00.

A	B
C	D
E	F

A Arcade Toy – Crane Co. – painted iron pedestal sink, $60.00 – 75.00.
B Crane Co., brass, $65.00 – 80.00.
C R.T. Crane – Brass & Bell Foundry, $80.00 – 95.00.
D Crane Bros. Mfg., metal, $45.00 – 60.00.
E Crane Co., 1855 – 1905, elephant, painted iron, trunk down, $70.00 – 85.00.
F Crane Co., 1855 – 1930, brass, Seventy-fifth anniversary, $20.00 – 30.00.

A	B	C
D	E	F
G	H	I

A   Hamilton Foundry, iron, $30.00 – 45.00.
B   Hamilton Foundry: 1891 – 1941, iron, $45.00 – 60.00.
C   Hamilton Foundry – Wolverine, rare, coated iron, $85.00 – 100.00.
D   Hamilton Foundry, anvil, stamped reverse side, plated iron, $60.00 – 75.00.
E   Hoosier Stoves, plated iron, $20.00 – 35.00.
F   Hoosier Stoves, iron, $25.00 – 40.00.
G   Hoosier Grain Drill Co. – Owl, rare, iron, $110.00 – 135.00.
H   Stove & Range Co. of Pittsburgh, iron, $45.00 – 60.00.
I   Hoosier Grain Drill Co. – Turtle, iron, $100.00 – 125.00.

A		B
C	D	E
F		

A Chicago, Milwaukee & St. Paul RR, bronze, $90.00 – 115.00.
B International Harvester – 1949, iron, $70.00 – 85.00.
C Coffee & Carkener Co., painted metal, $80.00 – 95.00.
D Grizzly Brake Lining, composition, $35.00 – 50.00.
E Parker Vises – Bear, enameled iron, $110.00 – 135.00.
F Parker Vises – Vise, iron, $125.00 – 150.00.

A	B	C
D	E	F
G	H	

A   Armour & Co. – pig, metal, $75.00 – 90.00.
B   Potts-Watkins-Walker: Illinois National Stock Yards, hog, metal, $100.00 – 125.00.
C   C.W. Stetson & Co., pig, iron, $65.00 – 80.00.
D   Colorado Fuel & Iron Co., pig, painted iron, $55.00 – 70.00.
E   Danville Stove Co. – 1898, beaver, iron, $60.00 – 75.00.
F   A. Pluemer & Co., pig, iron, $60.00 – 75.00.
G   Birmingham Iron Works, pig, iron, $15.00 – 25.00.
H   Bucki Carbon Ribbons, puppy, iron, $30.00 – 45.00.

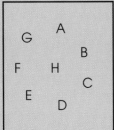

A   Armour & Co. – cow, plated metal, $75.00 – 90.00.
B   Pfaelzer Brothers, steer, coated bronze, advertising plate on reverse side, $85.00 – 100.00.
C   The Badger Mutual Fire Ins. Co., brass, $60.00 – 75.00.
D   Stamford Mfg. Co. – Tanning Extracts, steer, walnut brass, $85.00 – 100.00.
E   The Floyd-Wells Co. – Bengal Ranges, enameled iron, $150.00 – 200.00.
F   Frazer & Jones Co. – Saddlery, nickel brass, $130.00 – 160.00.
G   The Green Duck Co., painted iron, $65.00 – 80.00.
H   Deoxidized M. Co. – Owl Family, bronze, $65.00 – 80.00.

A   Union Porcelain Works, porcelain, $175.00 – 225.00.
B   Am. Electrical Heater Co., pencil holder, painted iron, marble base, $110.00 – 135.00.
C   Brillion Iron Works, painted iron, $60.00 – 75.00.
D   Merriam Segars, painted iron, $150.00 – 175.00.
E   The Dayton Caramel Works, glass eyes, metal, $200.00 – 250.00.
F   Phillips Foundry, brass, $65.00 – 80.00.
G   Littco Hardware, aluminum, $30.00 – 45.00.

A   Western Oil & Fuel Company, bronze, $100.00 – 125.00.
B   Lima Locomotive Works, painted iron, $150.00 – 175.00.
C   "Bulldog" Mutual Electric & Machine Co., painted metal, $125.00 – 150.00.
D   A.M. Greenblatt Studios – 1927, painted iron, $65.00 – 80.00.
E   Ace Foundry, brass, aluminum, $65.00 – 80.00.
F   Logan Bros. Grain Co., painted iron, brass, $80.00 – 95.00.

```
A   B   C
    D
E       F
```

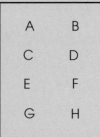

A   Consolidater Ice Co., metal, $75.00 – 90.00.
B   Wm. H. Sellards, bronze, $95.00 – 120.00.
C   Russian Co. – Romanoff Caviar – Sturgeon, rare, painted metal, $80.00 – 95.00.
D   Knox Stoves, "A Whale of a Stove," painted iron, $75.00 – 90.00.
E   Enterprise Ranges – Lobster, painted iron, $30.00 – 45.00.
F   Abbot Downing Co. – Wagons/Carriages, metal, $85.00 – 100.00.
G   BH Biscuits – mouse, metal, brass, $65.00 – 80.00.
H   Queen City Pattern Works – Rat, rare, metal, $190.00 – 220.00.

A   Benson's Wild Animal Farm – Nashua, N.H., painted iron, $75.00 – 90.00.
B   Armco: Spokane Culvert & Tank Co., metal, $60.00 – 75.00.
C   The Hancock Inspirator Co., bronze, ivory, $150.00 – 175.00.
D   Benson's Wild Animal Farm – Nashua, N.H., painted metal, $35.00 – 50.00.
E   The Phosphor Bronze Smelting Co., bronze, $65.00 – 80.00.
F   Independent Stove Co., plated iron, $90.00 – 120.00.
G   Crane Co.: 1855 – 1905, painted iron, elephant, trunk up, $70.00 – 85.00.
H   The Kelly Island Lime & Transport Co., painted metal, $60.00 – 75.00.

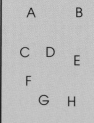

A   Monarch Fire Insurance Co., painted metal, $65.00 – 80.00.
B   Lone Star Bag – Bagging Co., plated metal, $30.00 – 45.00.
C   Franklin Bros. Co., metal, $20.00 – 35.00.
D   Lion Oil Refining Co., bronze, $110.00 – 135.00.
E   W.F. Molyneux Co., bronze, plated, $60.00 – 75.00.
F   Connell Pattern Machine Co., bronze, $35.00 – 50.00.
G   Fort Pitt Spring & Mfg. Co., metal, $20.00 – 30.00.
H   B.C. Wallace, metal, $15.00 – 25.00.

A Smidler's Drug Store, plated bronze, $70.00 – 85.00.
B Metro-Goldwyn-Mayer Lion, "The Greatest on the Screen," plated bronze, $85.00 – 100.00.
C Pointer Stoves & Ranges, iron match safe, $110.00 – 135.00.
D Dibert, Stark & Brown Cypress Co., iron, $65.00 – 80.00.
E Independent Stove Co., enameled iron, $35.00 – 50.00.
F Florida Title Co., plated bronze, $70.00 – 85.00.
G Carson Meyer & Co. Cigars/1891, not a match-safe iron, $200.00 – 250.00.

A   Sherwin Williams Co. – chameleon/palette, potmetal, iron, bronze, $200.00 – 250.00.
B   The Sherwin Williams Co. – chameleon, iron, $200.00 – 250.00.
C   M'Conway, Torley & Co., iron, frog, $110.00 – 135.00.
D   Redcut Tool Steel, brass, lizard, $70.00 – 85.00.
E   Red Star Oil, iron, lizard, $65.00 – 80.00.
F   McKenna Blue Chip, brass, $70.00 – 85.00.

A   Gestest-Toad, painted metal, $25.00 – 40.00.

B   Mohawk Tires, painted iron, $75.00 – 90.00.

C   C.I. Capps Co., male frog, iron, $60.00 – 75.00.

D   Superior Oxy. Acetylene Machine Co., painted iron, $60.00 – 75.00.

E   U. Grant Barr Fire Ins., celluloid/iron, hinged lid, $150.00 – 200.00.

F   Niagara Furnace F.C. F & M. Co., painted iron, $90.00 – 110.00.

G   Bernsteins Fish Grotto, celluloid/iron, $125.00 – 150.00.

H   Hunt-Helm-Ferris & Co., celluloid/iron, $100.00 – 125.00.

I   H.E. Garfield Injector Co. – 1891, bronze, $75.00 – 90.00.

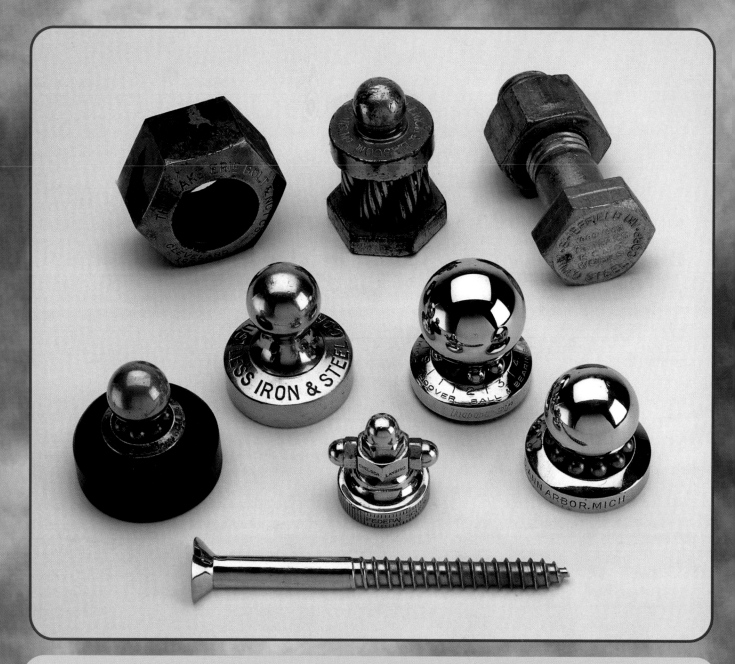

A The Lake Erie Bolt & Nut Co. – 1923, $25.00 – 35.00.
B Broderick & Bascom – Cable, $60.00 – 75.00.
C Armco. Steel Co. – Nut & Bolt, $20.00 – 30.00.
D Rustless Iron & Steel Corp., $50.00 – 65.00.
E Hoover Ball Bearing Co. – gambling/roulette, revolves, $80.00 – 95.00.
F Standard Roller Bearing Co., wood base revolves, $60.00 – 75.00.
G Federal Screw Works, revolves, $30.00 – 45.00.
H Hoover Ball Bearing – non-roulette, revolves, $60.00 – 75.00.
I Keeler Brass Co. – Wood Screws, $30.00 – 45.00.

A   Automatic Recording Safe Co. – egg safe, rare, painted brass, bottom embossed with company and product information, $100.00 – 125.00.
B   The Mosler Safe Co. – open book, rare, bronze, $120.00 – 145.00.
C   Cole Steel Equipment Co., felt bottom, $40.00 – 55.00.
D   The Mosler Safe Co., steel, Lucite base, $80.00 – 95.00.
E   Yale, bronze, felt bottom, $60.00 – 75.00.
F   Corbin Cabinet Lock Co., bottom embossed, Spanish-American War information on top, bronze, $90.00 – 110.00.
G   Independent Lock Co., painted iron, $110.00 – 135.00.

A   New York Bell System, $95.00 – 120.00.
B   Missouri & Kansas Telephone Co., reverse side, $110.00 – 135.00.
C   Louis F. Dow Co., plated brass, $35.00 – 50.00.
D   The C.S. Bell Co., iron, $100.00 – 125.00.
E   W.M. Bell & Co., brass, $35.00 – 50.00.
F   Revere & Son – 1816, painted iron, $20.00 – 30.00.
G   Liberty Foundry, iron, $30.00 – 45.00.
H   Chrysler – Three Billion 45 Cal. Bullet's Brass Bell w/Clapper – 1944,
    very rare, $175.00 – 225.00.

```
A  B  C

   D  E

F     H
   G
```

A   Southeast Mfg., iron, $25.00 – 40.00.
B   Bear Bearing Mfg. Co., bronze, $60.00 – 75.00.
C   Purdue Foundry, painted iron, $30.00 – 45.00.
D   R.D. Herbert & Sons Co., Nashville, Tenn., brass, $20.00 – 30.00.
E   L.A. Parker & Co., Evansville, Ind., brass, $20.00 – 30.00.
F   International Harvester, brass, $35.00 – 50.00.
G   Detroit Stove Works, nickel plated iron, $45.00 – 60.00.
H   Dorr Coke & Coal, bronze, $60.00 – 75.00.

A	B	C
D	E	F
G	H	

A   Chrysler 1928 – DeSoto – Plymouth, plated iron, $45.00 – 60.00.
B   Union Web, brass, $25.00 – 35.00.
C   Phoenix Pony Shoe, plated iron, $35.00 – 45.00.
D   Freidenberg & Speck — Tailors, bronze, $30.00 – 40.00.
E   Horsehill, painted iron, $25.00 – 40.00.
F   Diamond Tool and Horseshoe Co., plated iron, $25.00 – 40.00.
G   Never Slip Horseshoe Cleats, painted metal, $60.00 - 75.00.
H   Pedro Shoes, iron, $10.00 – 15.00.

A	B	
C	D	
E	F	G

A   Nor-Vell Sieve Co. – Sifter Sieves, brass, $80.00 – 95.00.
B   Channon-Emery Stove Co., iron, $60.00 – 75.00.
C   Endless Caverns — Campaign Hat, iron, $60.00 – 75.00.
D   Swigart Assoc. Insurance – decal matches embossment, painted iron, $125.00 – 150.00.
E   Juniata Valley Council – Boy Scouts of America, brass, $30.00 – 45.00.
F   The Eclipse Lawn Mower Co., iron, $75.00 – 90.00.
G   Standard Malleable Iron Co., iron, $45.00 – 60.00.

A   James E. Regan Importation Co./Shakespeare – Havana Cigars, bronze, composition base, $225.00 – 250.00.
B   Wolf, Sayer & Heller, pewter, hole in center for pencil, $225.00 – 275.00.
C   Fred S. Gichner – Iron Works, painted metal, $80.00 – 95.00.
D   El Reco Oil Co. – "Here's a Pal For You," painted iron, $75.00 – 90.00.
E   New York Edison Co. – 1922, bronze, $325.00 – 375.00.
F   The Dutch Boy Painter, metal, $100.00 – 125.00.

A   Delta Lumber Co., tree stump, painted iron, $90.00 – 110.00.
B   St. Louis Cooperage Co. – 1934, brass, $120.00 – 145.00.
C   Fairbanks Scales – 1930, plated brass, $80.00 – 95.00.
D   American Brake Shoe Co. – Tiger Bearings, bronze, $90.00 – 110.00.
E   Frost Lumber Industries, metal, $45.00 – 60.00.
F   Bridge & Leonard – Grain & Hay, painted metal, $70.00 – 85.00.

A	B	C
	D	
E	F	G

A   Associated Fire & Marine Ins. Co., metal, $45.00 – 60.00.
B   The Albert Dickenson Company – Pine Seeds, bronze, plated metal, pine tree, bags of seeds, $110.00 – 135.00.
C   Rosenau Bros. – Cinderella Frocks – 1939, metal, $60.00 – 75.00.
D   Attalla Pipe & Foundry Co., painted iron, $50.00 – 65.00.
E   Culmer Spring Co., brass, $65.00 – 80.00.
F   Syracuse Metals, plated metal, $35.00 – 50.00.
G   Buffalo Insurance Co., metal, $75.00 – 90.00.

A   S.W. Barnes & Son – Plumbing & Drainage, plated iron, $110.00 – 135.00.
B   H.G. Vogel Co. – Esty Sprinkler, rare, brass, $125.00 – 175.00.
C   Oil Well Supply Co., metal, $65.00 – 80.00.
D   The American Brass Co. – Anaconda, painted brass, $50.00 – 65.00.
E   Star Sprinkler Corp., nickeled brass, $75.00 – 90.00.
F   Eddy-Prescott – Fire Hydrants, painted iron, $80.00 – 95.00.
G   The Magee Carpet Co., metal dinner pail, $45.00 – 60.00.

A   B.F. Goodrich, aluminum, $25.00 – 40.00.
B   The Walkover Shoe – Princess, metal, $50.00 – 65.00.
C   Cammeyer's Shoe Store, plated iron, $80.00 – 95.00.
D   Mueller Faucets, steel, $90.00 – 110.00.
E   F. Merten's Sons, metal, $40.00 – 55.00.
F   Kalak Water Co. – Alkaline, metal, $40.00 – 55.00.
G   Adjustable Clamp Co., tin base, iron or steel clamp, $35.00 – 50.00.
H   Star Expansion Bolt Co., bronze, $75.00 – 90.00.

A   B   C
    E
D   F   G
    H

	A
F	B
	G
E	C
	D

A   Rip Van Winkle Salt, iron, $75.00 – 90.00.
B   Golden F & M Co., iron, $70.00 – 85.00.
C   Thatcher – Ranges & Furnaces, bronzed plated iron, $65.00 – 80.00.
D   Chesterfield Pipe Fitters, iron, $100.00 – 125.00.
E   S.B. Penick & Co. – Drugs – Hippocrates, painted metal, $65.00 – 80.00.
F   Cash's Woven Names, iron, $85.00 – 105.00.
G   B & B Mfg. Co., nickeled whistle, $70.00 – 85.00.

A   Atlas Casket Co., metal, $100.00 – 125.00.
B   Pioneer Pipe Line Co., metal, $60.00 – 75.00.
C   The American Chain Co., metal, $110.00 – 135.00.
D   Vulcan Rail & Construction Co., metal, $70.00 – 85.00.
E   Hercules Cement, metal, $40.00 – 55.00.
F   The Globe Co. – Equipment, metal, $80.00 – 95.00.
G   William Jaeger – Artistic Lamps, bronze Victorian lady, $95.00 – 120.00.

A	B	C
D	E	F
	G	

A   C.C. Spink & Son, painted metal, $40.00 – 55.00.
B   Royal Stoves, painted iron, A.C. Williams Toy Co., $75.00 – 90.00.
C   Kewanee Boiler Co., painted metal, $100.00 – 125.00.
D   Reid Brothers – Moderate Priced Tailors, painted iron, $150.00 – 200.00.
E   Millett Brass Co., brass, $70.00 – 85.00.
F   Jos. M. Hayes Woolen Co. – Tailors Trimmings, iron, $175.00 – 225.00.
G   Massengill – Safeiron, painted iron, $35.00 – 50.00.

A	B	C
	D	E	
F	G	H

A   The Indiana Engraving Co., metal, $25.00 – 35.00.
B   Rolls Royce – Grill, metal, $100.00 – 125.00.
C   The Crescent Engraving Co., metal, $25.00 – 35.00.
D   Virginia Soapstone Co., metal soapstone, $30.00 – 45.00.
E   New Hall Chain Forge & Iron Co., metal, $80.00 – 95.00.
F   The Art Stove Co. – The Laurel, nickeled iron, $35.00 – 50.00.
G   Western Washer Mfg. Co., steel, $20.00 – 35.00.
H   Deeley Iron Works, bronze, $40.00 – 55.00.

A   Doran – Seattle, Wa., bronze, $65.00 – 80.00.
B   Sheriffs – Milwaukee, Wi. – C.W. Moore, bronze, $50.00 – 65.00.
C   Doll's Garage Inc. – Pontiac, metal, $90.00 – 115.00.
D   RCA – Parts & Accessories, brass, $60.00 – 75.00.
E   The American Envelope Co., bronze, $65.00 – 80.00.
F   Buffalo Envelope Co., brass, $45.00 – 60.00.

A	B
C	D
E	F

A   American Meter Company, painted metal, $60.00 – 75.00.
B   The Reeves Mfg. Co., painted metal, $70.00 – 85.00.
C   Wayne Oil Burner, painted metal, $45.00 – 60.00.
D   National Cash Register, iron, $55.00 – 70.00.
E   R.C. Allen – Adding Machines, painted metal, $30.00 – 45.00.
F   York Compressors – level on top, painted metal, $40.00 – 55.00.
G   York Engines, iron, $45.00 – 60.00.
H   R. Hoe & Co. – Presses, metal, $25.00 – 40.00.

A	B	C
D	E	F
G	H	

	A	B	C
	D	E	F
			G

A Maryland Meter Mfg. Co. – The American Gas Light Assoc., 1889 Excursion, brass, $80.00 – 95.00.

B Westinghouse Electric – Light bulb, brass, silverplated base and threads, $70.00 – 85.00.

C Carry-Lite Decoys, weighted papier-mache, $120.00 – 145.00.

D S.S. California – Panama Pacific Line, rare, metal alabaster base, $175.00 – 225.00.

E Old Line Auto Insurors, iron-brass, cloisonne, $125.00 – 150.00.

F Wm. Harris & Co. – Mine Car Hitchings & Forgings, metal/ivory dice, $90.00 – 110.00.

G Westinghouse Electric, brass, $40.00 – 55.00.

A   Chicago World's Fairs – 1893 & 1933 – globe & base revolve, metal, $70.00 – 85.00.
B   Universal Studios – California, painted metal, $80.00 – 95.00.
C   Italian Line – Anchor, painted brass, $80.00 – 95.00.
D   Century of Progress – Chicago 1933 – Sabre Tooth Tiger, bronze, $115.00 – 140.00.
E   T.S.F. Photo – S.A.R.R.E. – Paris, painted copper, $125.00 – 150.00.
F   Century of Progress – Chicago 1933, burwood composition, $30.00 – 45.00.

A	B
C	D
E	F

A   B.B. Line, metal, $35.00 – 50.00.
B   Archer Prescription Shop, bronze, bow missing – rare, $75.00 – 90.00.
C   H.R. Mining & Smelting Co., howling wolf, zinc, $30.00 – 45.00.
D   Sterling Boat Engines, metal, $35.00 – 50.00.
E   J.C. MacElroy Co. – Steel Products, aluminum bollard, $45.00 – 60.00.
F   Penn Hdw., iron, $30.00 – 45.00.
G   Buckwalter Stove Co., nickeled iron, $65.00 – 70.00.

A   B   C

D   E

F

G

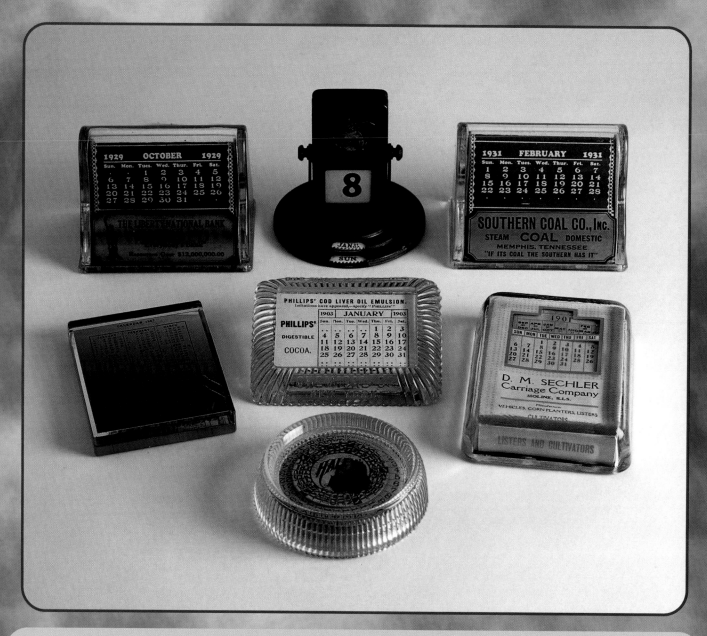

All calendars.
A The Liberty National Bank – 1929, roll calendar, glass, $35.00 – 50.00.
B GMAC Plan – perpetual, metal, $20.00 – 30.00.
C Southern Coal Co. – 1931, glass, roll calendar, $35.00 – 50.00.
D Cunard Line – 1957 & 1958, glass, $20.00 – 30.00.
E Chas. H. Phillips Chemical Co. 1903 – 1906, glass, $75.00 – 90.00.
F D.M. Sechler – Carriage Co. – perpetual, glass, $80.00 – 95.00.
G Haley's Writing Inks – perpetual, glass, $80.00 – 95.00.

A	B	C
D	E	F
G		

All thermometers.
A Parkwood Pharmacy, $50.00 – 65.00.
B Terre Haute Advertising Co., $15.00 – 25.00.
C Rockford Varnish Co., $75.00 – 90.00.
D Consol Coal – Honeywell, $35.00 – 50.00.
E F.B. Rogers Silver Co., $30.00 – 45.00.
F National Mill Supply – Honeywell, $35.00 – 50.00.
G Pennsylvania Coroners – Honeywell, $35.00 – 50.00.

```
    A     B
            C
    D   E   F
    G
```

A   Christian International Ltd., Lucite, real oil inside, $60.00 – 75.00.
B   Lipton Tea Co., Lucite, teapot, cup and saucer, and Lipton tea bag, $80.00 – 95.00.
C   G.W. Sullivant Geologist Producer, Lucite, wells listed, real oil inside, $60.00 – 75.00.
D   Independent Bankers Assoc., Lucite, $45.00 – 60.00.
E   United States Fidelity & Guaranty Co., Bakelite, $35.00 – 50.00.

A	B
C	D
E	F

A   W.W. Wattles & Sons, 1492 – 1892, porcelain, $200.00 – 250.00.
B   Southern Steel Co., porcelain, $25.00 – 40.00.
C   Clairmont Trucking, porcelain, $25.00 – 40.00.
D   Westron Corporation, porcelain, $25.00 – 40.00.
E   Western Stoneware Co., glazed stoneware, $45.00 – 60.00.
F   The Colorado Bedding Co. – Monobat Mattresses, ceramic,
       $60.00 – 75.00.

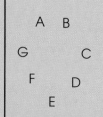

A   Perry & Morrill – General Contractors, plastic, $20.00 – 30.00.

B   Berkshire Ins., painted iron, $100.00 – 125.00.

C   Brunswick – D.C.B., real eight-ball, $60.00 – 75.00.

D   Martins Gymnasium Equipment Co., plastic, $25.00 – 35.00.

E   Westclox – Celestial Paperweight Clock, glass, metal, and composition numeral bezel, $75.00 – 90.00.

F   I.C.B. Tournament – St. Louis 1937, plated metal, $30.00 – 45.00.

G   H.A. Stahl Real Estate Co., painted iron, $90.00 – 110.00.

A   Greyhound Bus Executive Desk Paperweight, bronze, $80.00 – 95.00.
B   Brownie Baking Co., painted aluminum, $45.00 – 60.00.
C   Howell "Redband" Motors, iron, $30.00 – 45.00.
D   Sears, painted metal, $30.00 – 45.00.
E   Anderson Buick Co., ABC Buick, note holder, metal, $30.00 – 50.00.
F   Acker Cement Works – "Waylite Blocks," metal, $30.00 – 45.00.
G   Chemical Paper Mfg. Co., cloisonné brass, $30.00 – 45.00.
H   Johnson Sea Horse, painted iron, $35.00 – 50.00.

A	B	C
D	E	F
G	H	

All lead.
A   National Lead Co. – Genuine Babbitt Metal, $20.00 – 40.00.
B   National Lead Co. – Solder Dutch Boy 888, $20.00 – 40.00.
C   National Lead Co. – Heavy Pressure Metal, $20.00 – 40.00.
D   National Lead Co. – Phoenix Metal, $20.00 – 40.00.
E   National Lead Co. – Perfection Anti-Friction Metal, $20.00 – 40.00.
F   National Lead Co. – Sterling Journal Metal, $20.00 – 40.00.

A   Kennedy & Sons – Chromang – Ontario, nickled iron, $30.00 – 45.00.
B   Waukeska Nickel – Canada, nickel, $60.00 – 75.00.
C   Darling Bros. Ltd. – Elevators Etc. – Montreal, brass, $25.00 – 40.00.
D   Nisbet & Auld Ltd. – Toronto, bronze, $60.00 – 75.00.
E   Warde Kinge & Sons – Hotwater Boilers – Montreal, glass,
    $30.00 – 45.00.
F   Canada Cycle & Motor Co. – Bicycles – Skates – Toronto, nickel
    bronze, $200.00 – 225.00.

A   Central Mfg. Co., painted iron, $85.00 – 100.00.
B   GMC "The Truck of Extra Value," metal, $80.00 – 95.00.
C   Yukevich Motor Sales – Pontiac, metal, $75.00 – 90.00.
D   J.H. Holan Corp., metal, $60.00 – 75.00.

A	B
C	D

A	A Fairbanks-Morse Co. – Diesel Engines, metal, $100.00 – 125.00.
B	B Beloit Iron Works, metal, $65.00 – 80.00.
C	C The Cleveland Twist Drill Co., bronze, used to hold drill bits in machine shops, $85.00 – 110.00.
D	D John L. Bobo & Co. – Capitol Brand, metal, $110.00 – 135.00.

A   G.M. Diehl Machine Works, metal, $85.00 – 110.00.
B   Regal Typewriter Co. – "Royal," metal, top lifts, compartment inside,
    $80.00 – 100.00.
C   Smith Bros. Cough Drops – "Star" on reverse side, painted iron,
    $50.00 – 65.00.
D   Electric Railway Equipment Co., bronze, $175.00 – 225.00.
E   Radio News – "Read Radio News," news stand paper "weight,"
    original, reproductions made in 1980s, painted iron, rare, $85.00 – 110.00.

A	B
C	
D	E

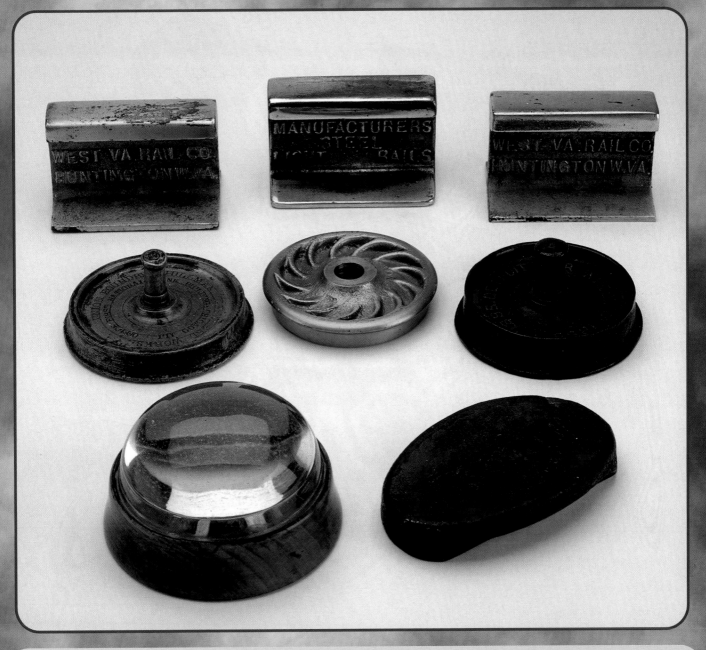

A   West Virginia Rail Co. – Rails – Switches, Ties, Shapes, Bars, nickel steel, $60.00 – 75.00.

B   West Virginia Rail Co. – Light Steel Rails, nickel steel, $60.00 – 75.00.

C   West Virginia Rail Co. Mine Ties, Frogs & Switches, nickel steel, $60.00 – 75.00.

D   Union Foundry & Pullman Car Wheel Works, bronze, $150.00 – 175.00.

E   St. Louis Southern Railroad – reverse side, brass, $70.00 – 85.00.

F   Detroit Car Wheel Co., 1885, bronze, $125.00 – 150.00.

G   Barkalow Bros. Railway News Contractors, glass-wood base, minerals, $25.00 – 40.00.

H   B & O Railroad, painted iron, $45.00 – 60.00.

A General American Tank Car Corp., metal iron base, $80.00 – 95.00.
B Kansas City Southern Lines, steel, $35.00 – 50.00.
C Havana Coal Company, bronze, $100.00 – 125.00.
D National Molasses Company, usually attached to a note pad holder, metal, $60.00 – 75.00.
E PRR – Pennsylvania Railroad, iron, $70.00 – 85.00.
F Asbestos & Magnesia Mfg. Co. – Locomotive Lagging, brass, $120.00 – 145.00.

A	B
C	D
E	F

All metal.
A   New York Central 20th Century – Hudson "Type" Locomotive, $110.00 – 135.00.
B   New York Central – Hudson "Type" Locomotive, $90.00 – 115.00.
C   Evans, Stillman & Co. – First New York Central Train 1831, $65.00 – 80.00.
D   Strasburg Railroad, $15.00 – 30.00.
E   British Empire Expo. London 1924, Largest Passenger Locomotive in the World, $80.00 – 95.00.

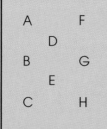

A   Ben Williams, wood knob, iron, $45.00 – 60.00.
B   Cumner Jones & Co., iron, $45.00 – 60.00.
C   E.W. Blatchford Co. – Metals, metal, $35.00 – 50.00.
D   Excelsior Stove & Mfg. Co., reverse side – National Stoves, nickeled iron, $90.00 – 110.00.
E   Peabody, Houghteling & Co. – 1865, brass, $45.00 – 60.00.
F   Samuel Noyes & Son – Tailors, iron, $45.00 – 60.00.
G   Von Borries & Co. – Tailors, Woolens, brass, $40.00 – 55.00.
H   Frank W. Greaves & Co., nickeled iron, $50.00 – 65.00.

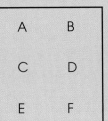

A	B
C	D
E	F
G	

A U.S. Malt Co., brass, $35.00 – 50.00.

B The Battery Park National Bank, brass, $30.00 – 45.00.

C Commercial Electrical Supply Co., brass, $30.00 – 45.00.

D Old Dominion Building & Loan, brass, $65.00 – 80.00.

E The Washington Life Insurance Co., bronze iron, $65.00 – 80.00.

F The St. Clair Plating Co., iron, $45.00 – 60.00.

G Alan Wood Iron & Steel Co., nickeled iron, $45.00 – 60.00.

A   Alamo Iron Works – 1878, iron, $30.00 – 45.00.
B   Alburger, Stoer & Co. Tailors, 1876 "Weight & Clip," nickeled metal, $60.00 – 75.00.
C   Purdue Foundry, iron, $30.00 – 45.00.
D   The Karl Kiefer Multiple Perfection Beer Filter, brass iron, $65.00 – 80.00.
E   La Paluma Fruit Co., metal, $45.00 – 60.00.
F   The Billings & Spencer Co. – Forgings, nickeled brass, $60.00 – 75.00.
G   Alburger, Stoer & Co. – lizard, nickeled iron, $100.00 – 125.00.

A	B	C
	D	E	
	F	G	

	A	
B		C
D		E
F		G

A   Gra-Iron Fdry. Corp., iron, $60.00 – 75.00.
B   Byers "Bearcat" Crane, nickeled iron, $45.00 – 60.00.
C   Maine Man'g Refrigerators – White Mountain, nickeled iron, $45.00 – 60.00.
D   Maine Man'g Refrigerators – White Mountain, nickeled iron, $45.00 – 60.00.
E   North Bros. Mfg. Co., bronze, $60.00 – 75.00.
F   Knothe Brothers – Belts & Suspenders, iron, $60.00 – 75.00.
G   Kraeuter & Co. – Tools & Forgings, iron, $85.00 – 100.00.

All bronze, three-footed.
A   The Franklin Fire Insurance Co. – 1919, $75.00 – 90.00.
B   Wm. H. Horstmann Co. – 1916, $85.00 – 100.00.
C   J. Gibson McIlvain Co. – Lumber – 1923, $45.00 – 60.00.
D   The Capitol Fuel Co., $40.00 – 55.00.
E   Blodgett & Orswell Co. – Threads, $75.00 – 90.00.
F   United States Trust Co. – 1927, $50.00 – 65.00.
G   Canal National Bank – 1826, $35.00 – 50.00.
H   Moshier Bros. – 1927 – Vanilla Extracts, $60.00 – 75.00.

A	B
C	D
E	F
G	H

All bronze, four-footed.

A Fritzsche Brothers – 1921, $50.00 – 65.00.

B The Real Estate Title Ins. & Trust Co. – 1926, $60.00 – 75.00.

C Dort Motor Car Co., company folded in 1924, car shown is a 1923 6-cylinder, $110.00 – 135.00.

D The Bead Chain Mfg. Co. (cloisonné), $70.00 – 85.00.

E N.W. Ayer & Co. – 1919, $45.00 – 60.00.

F Chalmers Motor Co., $80.00 – 95.00.

G Cameron Appliance Co. – Cable Rings, $70.00 – 85.00.

H J. Spencer Turner Co. – U.S. Army Duck, $70.00 - 85.00.

A	B	C
	D	E
	F	G

A   American Insurance Group – 1946, $45.00 – 60.00.
B   Pawtucket Mutual Fire Ins. Co. – 1948, bronze, two-footed, $60.00 – 75.00.
C   The Connecticut Fire Ins. Co. – 1950 – P.W. Burns, bronze, two-footed, $45.00 – 60.00.
D   New York World's Fair – 1940 – Auto Race, 3rd Place, bronze, $75.00 – 85.00.
E   Peter A. Frasse & Co., 1816 – 1941 – Robt. Fulton's Steamboat, bronze, $70.00 – 85.00.
F   American Automobile Ins. Co., bronze, $80.00 – 95.00.
G   The Delaware & Hudson Co. – 1929 – "The Stourbridge" Lion, bronze, $75.00 – 90.00.

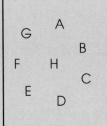

All bronze.
A   G.AR. 39th National Encampment – Pikes Peak – 1905, $45.00 – 60.00.
B   Central Mfg.'s Mutual Ins. Co. – 1876 – "Chief" the Dog, $65.00 – 80.00.
C   Columbian Rope Co. – 1953 – Colonel Metcalf, $35.00 – 50.00.
D   St. Louis Southwestern Railway – Cotton Belt Route, $65.00 – 80.00.
E   The AT. Stearns Lumber Co. – 1924, $65.00 – 80.00.
F   William Skinner & Son – Ames Sword Co., bronze, $100.00 – 125.00.
G   Prudential Ins. Co. of America – 1925, $50.00 – 65.00.
H   William Skinner & Son – 1923 – Silks & Satins, three-footed, brass $75.00 – 90.00.

<table>
<tr><td>A</td><td>H.J. Heinz Co. – 1939, bronze, $35.00 – 50.00.</td></tr>
<tr><td>B</td><td>Baush & Lomb Optical Co. – 1928, bronze, $60.00 – 75.00.</td></tr>
<tr><td>C</td><td>New York & Boston Steamer – Cape Cod Canal, metal, $15.00 – 25.00.</td></tr>
<tr><td>D</td><td>Navy Yard Boston – 1936 – U.S.S. Mugford, U.S.S. Ralph Talbot, bronze, $50.00 – 65.00.</td></tr>
<tr><td>E</td><td>U.S.S. Monaghan – 1935, bronze, $45.00 – 60.00.</td></tr>
<tr><td>F</td><td>The Chicago Lumber Co. – 1951, bronze, $60.00 – 75.00.</td></tr>
<tr><td>G</td><td>Maritime Assoc. of the Port of New York – 1919, metal, $60.00 – 75.00.</td></tr>
<tr><td>H</td><td>James W. Elwell & Co. – 1921, bronze, four-footed, $65.00 – 80.00.</td></tr>
</table>

Key diagram:

```
A  B  C
    E
 D  F
 G  H
```

A Ajax Metal Co. – Bull Alloy, plated metal, $35.00 – 50.00.
B Continental Cream Separator – "Dixie," bronze, $35.00 – 50.00.
C Rhode Island Fittings Co., bronze, $25.00 – 40.00.
D Revere Copper & Brass Products, brass, $25.00 – 40.00.
E Bentonville Casting Co., iron, $20.00 – 35.00.
F The Carlisle & Finch Co. – Search Lights, iron, $35.00 – 50.00.
G The L.J. Farnum Dies – 1916, dental impressions, brass, $50.00 – 65.00.
H Vonnegut Machinery Co., brass, $40.00 – 55.00.

A	B	C
D	E	F
G	H	

A   R.H. Hood Co. Comb Circles, glass, bronze, three-footed, $60.00 – 75.00.
B   The Cleveland & Western Coal Co., bronze, $45.00 – 60.00.
C   Benj. Harris & Co., bronze, $20.00 – 35.00.
D   Titan Metal Mfg. Co. – 1915, brass, $15.00 – 25.00.
E   Des Moines Stove Repair Co. – 1869, iron, $25.00 – 40.00.
F   Indian River Oranges & Grapefruit – Florigold, brass, $35.00 – 50.00.
G   General Electric, brass, $25.00 – 40.00.
H   Gold Star Oil Burner Mfg. Co., bronze, $50.00 – 65.00.

A	B
C	D E
F	G H

A	B	C
D	E	F
G	H	I

A Norton Lashier Co. – Door Closers, iron, $15.00 – 25.00.
B Joseph Glenn & Sons – Leather Belts, iron, $15.00 – 25.00.
C Shannon & Co. – Tools & Railroad Supplies, iron, $15.00 – 25.00.
D Shannon & Co. – Contractors Equipment, iron, $15.00 – 25.00.
E Service Supply Corp. – Industrial Supplies, iron, $15.00 – 25.00.
F Penn Hardware Co. – Locks, iron, $30.00 – 45.00.
G Pratt & Whitney Engines – "McConnell," aluminum, $35.00 – 50.00.
H M.W. Hartmann Mfg. Co. – Foundry, painted iron, $15.00 – 30.00.
I Mack – Crank Shaft, steel, $35.00 – 50.00.

A K.G.R. 1909 – Eagle, painted iron, $30.00 – 45.00.
B Dillner Moving & Transfer Co., glass, $65.00 – 80.00.
C The Dexter Foundry, iron, $15.00 – 25.00.
D H.L. Buss Company – Shippers, composition, $30.00 – 45.00.
E United American Metals – Stonewall Babbitt, metal, $20.00 – 35.00.
F R.R. Donnelley & Sons Co. – Lakeside Press, copper, $20.00 – 35.00.
G Old Hickory – Babbitt Metal, painted metal, $20.00 – 35.00.

A	B
C	D
E	F	G

A   Welch Hustlebur, bronze, $20.00 – 25.00.
B   Boy Scout Oath – medallion "spins," metal, $25.00 – 40.00.
C   Early Boy Scout Emblem, iron, $30.00 – 45.00.
D   Fort Snelling, military outpost, built in 1825, painted iron, $15.00 – 25.00.
E   The C.H. Hanson Co. – name & data plates, metal, $35.00 – 50.00.
F   Parke-Davis "Tabron" Prenatal Vitamins, pewter, $60.00 – 75.00.
G   BSA – Cub Scouts – Wolf, bronze, $20.00 – 35.00.

A	B	C
D	E	F
G		

A Red Cross "4 gallons," O. Wendell Lynch, aluminum, $15.00 – 25.00.
B Moczik Tool & Die Works, aluminum, $35.00 – 50.00.
C Simplex Vises, Desmond Dressers & Cutters, metal, $20.00 – 35.00.
D Shenandoah, Pa. – coal, souvenir, $20.00 – 35.00.
E W.H. Ewing Furriers – Newfoundland, seal skin, $25.00 – 40.00.
F Templeton Kenly Co. – Simplex Jacks, metal, $20.00 – 35.00.
G Coal Breaker – coal, souvenir, $25.00 – 40.00.

All souvenirs.
A   Fort Leavenworth – 1827, $15.00 – 25.00.
B   Dodge City, Kansas – Boot Hill, $35.00 – 50.00.
C   Quincy Mine #2 Suitcase – Hancock, Mich., $20.00 – 35.00.
D   Hershey, Pa., $20.00 – 35.00.
E   Municipal Pier "Navy Pier" – Chicago, $25.00 – 40.00.
F   Adler Planetarium – Chicago, $20.00 – 35.00.
G   Iowa State Capitol – iron turtle, celluloid, $40.00 – 60.00.
H   Municipal Airport "Midway" – Chicago, $90.00 – 115.00.
I   The Hitching Post – Kentucky Lake – Turtle, shaking head & legs, $30.00 – 45.00.

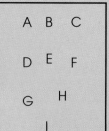

All souvenirs.
A   Inclined Plane – Johnstown, Pa., $15.00 – 25.00.
B   Teachers College – Kansas City, Mo., $20.00 – 35.00.
C   Boston – pot of baked beans, $20.00 – 35.00.
D   New York World's Fair – 1940, $30.00 – 45.00.
E   Manitou & Pikes Peak Railway, $15.00 – 25.00.
F   Regency Inn – Key West, Fla., $10.00 – 20.00.
G   Maine – iron lobster, $20.00 – 35.00.
H   Cape Cod, Mass. – iron lobster, $20.00 – 35.00.
I   Empire State Bldg. – NYC, $20.00 – 35.00.

A   Fontana Dam, N.C. – calendar, souvenir, $20.00 – 35.00.
B   I.R.L.C.A State Convention – U.S. Mail, painted iron, $25.00 – 40.00.
C   Boyertown Caskets, bronze, $100.00 – 125.00.
D   Batesville Caskets, composition, $45.00 – 60.00.
E   Ohio Electric Controller Co. – industrial magnet, painted metal, $25.00 – 40.00.
F   Neptune Meter Co. – Trident, wood base, brass, $20.00 – 35.00.
G   John Wright – made figural bottle openers, painted iron turtle, $35.00 – 50.00.

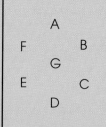

A   Active Fortune – Specialty Furnaces – ashtray, painted iron, $15.00 – 25.00.
B   Machinist Co. Glen E. Gear, iron, $15.00 – 25.00.
C   Haag's Hotel – Shartlesville, Pa. – pretzel, painted iron, $10.00 – 20.00.
D   Graybill – Fixtures – note holder, metal & celluloid, $20.00 – 35.00.
E   Ulysses S. Grant – President & Civil War General, painted iron, $25.00 – 40.00.
F   Josaw Products Foundry Co., brass, $15.00 – 25.00.
G   Reading Hardware Co., ashtray, iron, $20.00 – 35.00.

A   American Can Co. – keglined beer cans, tin, $25.00 – 40.00.
B   Drewrys Ale – keglined, tin, souvenir, $25.00 – 40.00.
C   Regroton – Drug, metal, $15.00 – 25.00.
D   Cushman & Denison Mfg. Co., pen & pencil holder, glass,
    $15.00 – 20.00.
E   Cory Filters, glass, $15.00 – 20.00.
F   Early twelve-sided Las Vegas Casino Cube, plastic, some casinos
    shown are no longer there, Sands, Dunes, Landmark, $15.00 – 20.00.
G   Sakrete Concrete Mixes, $15.00 – 25.00.
H   Hermitage Portland Cement, cement, $10.00 – 15.00.

A   Acmes Iron Co. – Mine Car, $35.00 – 50.00.
B   The Stanley Works – Hinges, salesman's sample, opens, wood, brass,
      $75.00 – 90.00.
C   Eagle – Horseshoe – crest HP, painted iron, $10.00 – 20.00.
D   Back embossed Beards Pub, lobster, very old, original red paint, iron,
      $70.00 – 85.00.

A	B
C	D

A	B	C
	D	
E	F	

All non-advertising.
A   Victorian, rectangle, brass, iron, $40.00 – 65.00.
B   Inlaid, turned & weighted, round, ebony, $50.00 – 65.00.
C   Victorian, octagon, iron, $60.00 – 75.00.
D   Victorian, rectangle, iron, $35.00 – 50.00.
E   "Acorn" shape finial, round, brass, $35.00 – 50.00.
F   Bank tellers paperweight, oval, iron, $30.00 – 45.00.

All non-advertising.
A   Head on base – unknown famous person, possibly a young Abe Lincoln, painted iron, $35.00 – 50.00.
B   Book Press, painted iron, $90.00 – 110.00.
C   Golf Ball – square base, painted iron, $85.00 – 100.00.
D   Baseball – infield, painted iron, $125.00 – 150.00.
E   Golf Ball – round base, painted iron, $70.00 – 85.00.
F   Cigar, iron, $45.00 – 60.00.

A Plow, steel, non-advertising, $50.00 – 65.00.
B Jeweler's anvil – O.W.B. Steel, iron, $30.00 – 45.00.
C Bulldog match holder & striker, bronze, non-advertising, $110.00 – 135.00.
D Knife on rocks – Anagram, brass, $80.00 – 95.00.
E Lizard, brass, non-advertising, $90.00 – 110.00.
F Lizard on round base, brass, onyx, non-advertising, $45.00 – 60.00.

```
A  B  C

   D

E     F
```

A   Optometrist Eye, "I've Got My Eye on You," porcelain, rubber plug,
    $65.00 – 80.00.
B   Inkwell for Quills – ground & polished glass base, brass screw-in funnel
    top, non-advertising, $100.00 – 125.00.
C   Ben Franklin, bronze, $65.00 – 80.00.
D   Dice thermometer – France, brass, $35.00 – 50.00.
E   A White Friar's Paperweight Inkwell, ground & polished bottom, circa
    1840 (*Lyle Antiques Review* 1987), non-advertising, $500.00+. If later
    Japanese made, value much less.
F   Victorian "Weight & Clip" – 1876, iron, non-advertising, $60.00 – 75.00.

A   R.C. Allen – Typewriter, metal, $35.00 – 50.00.
B   Atlas Mattress Co. – Abraham Lincoln, composition, $35.00 – 50.00.
C   S & S Chevrolet Co. – Scale Queen, aluminum & plastic, $25.00 – 45.00.
D   Allied Laboratories – Scale Queen, aluminum & plastic, $25.00 – 45.00.
E   Norddeutscher Lloyd – Kaiser Wilhelm II, metal, $75.00 – 95.00.
F   Brown Chemical Co., bronzed metal, $20.00 – 35.00.
G   Five Boro Cab, painted metal, $15.00 – 30.00.

A   B & M Smelter – Great Falls, Montana, metal, $125.00 – 150.00.
B   Curtis Paper Co., metal, $85.00 – 100.00.
C   Woodruff & Edwards Inc., iron, $65.00 – 80.00.
D   Kendallville Foundry Inc., plated iron, $60.00 – 75.00.
E   Empire Brushes "Clean Around the World," metal, $50.00 – 65.00.
F   United States Fuel Co., metal, $225.00 – 275.00.

A	B	C
D	E	F

A   Frank Lucas – 1855 Austria, plated iron, $65.00 – 80.00.
B   Macklanburg Duncan Co., hat, brass, $70.00 – 85.00.
C   Briggs Hoffmann, celluloid, mirror, $55.00 – 70.00.
D   Dempster – frog, painted iron, $65.00 – 80.00.
E   Moran Towing Corp., Curtis Bay – reverse, metal, $25.00 – 40.00.
F   Giant Grip Mfg. Co., horseshoe, 1863 – 1938, painted iron, $20.00 – 35.00.

A   Reading Traffic Club 1953 – Reading RR employees, metal, $65.00 – 80.00.

B   C.H. Packwood – "Pax" Skin Cleansers, ashtray, rooster and ashtray screw together, embossed bottom, has product company info, brass, $80.00 – 95.00.

C   Clark-Gandion Co. – Surgical Instruments, metal, $65.00 – 80.00.

D   AMCT – campaign hat, painted iron, $35.00 – 50.00.

E   Universal Microphone Co. – Kore/Kido, metal, $65.00 – 80.00.

F   C.I. Capps – female frog, brass, $65.00 – 80.00.

A	B	C
D	E	F

A   International Carriers – Calvin Bullock, New York Central – Hudson Metal,
     $85.00 – 110.00.
B   Victorian, octagon, iron, non-advertising, $60.00 – 75.00.
C   Bank tellers paperweight, oval, iron, non-advertising, $30.00 – 45.00.
D   Electrical Ship Building Industry, ashtray, Belgium, brass/copper,
     $60.00 – 75.00.
E   Victorian, octagon, iron, non-advertising, $60.00 – 75.00.
F   Hamilton Standard – Propellers/Aircraft, brass, $45.00 – 60.00.

	A B C
	D F
	E
	G

A   Indian Head Casket Co., copper-plated iron, $125.00 – 175.00.
B   Mariner's Savings Bank – 1927, sperm whale, iron, $70.00 – 85.00.
C   Detroit Float & Stamping Co., copper & iron, $75.00 – 90.00.
D   Astor Exterminating Co., Terminix Co. of Mass., rare, brass, wings lift, recessed body, $175.00 – 225.00.
E   Use Peerless Products – lizard, painted iron, $65.00 – 80.00.
F   Pontiac, sixes & eights, painted metal, $75.00 – 95.00.
G   National Lock Co., wood & brass, $85.00 – 110.00.

A   Birmingham Title and Guaranty Co., milk glass appearance on back, $70.00 – 85.00.

B   Steamer "Theodore Roosevelt" – Chicago, weighted celluloid, $45.00 – 60.00.

C   Garcia & Vega Habana Cigars, rare, finished iron, three cigars are attached, one mold, $150.00 – 175.00.

D   D & B "Queen of the Lakes" Steamer Eastern States, tinback, 5 dice, $100.00 – 125.00.

E   Pekin Cooperage Co. 1915, vitrolite, milk glass, Panama Canal calendar, very rare, $175.00 – 225.00.

F   Panama Mail Steamship Co. – Propeller, bronze, all three blades stamped, $65.00 – 80.00.

A   Hartford Sewing Machine, $10.00.
B   New Hampton General Store, $10.00.
C   Blue Mountain Lake, Adirondack Mts., $10.00.
D   Chesapeake & Ohio Railway, $10.00.
E   Burdock Blood Bitters, $10.00.
F   Home Manufacturing Co., $10.00.
G   Madeira – Cutlery, $10.00.
H   Solar Tip Shoes, $10.00.
I   Steamer Chippewa, $10.00.
J   Beck J. Meyer, $10.00.

A	B
C	D
E	F
G	H
I	J

About the Authors

Dick Holiner

Dick Holiner was born in Chicago, Illinois, where his father was in the hotel business and taught him his love for the outdoors, which Dick still enjoys today, making fishing trips each year to South America and Mexico. During his youth Dick traveled with his parents to Europe before the second World War. Later he attended the University of Miami and served a military tour of duty in Korea during the 1950s. He managed a Holiday Inn in Indiana and a resort in Islamorada in the Florida Keys where the film crew of a movie about John F. Kennedy and PT109 were among his guests.

For years he worked for a CBS affiliate television station in Henderson, Kentucky, where he helped start a fishing show which today is the popular "Fishin' Hole" on the ESPN network.

Dick has authored books on antique locks, barber bottles, and purses. He now lives near Nashville, Tenn. where he buys antiques for two restaurant chains, Cracker Barrel and T.G.I. Friday's. He continues to write about and collect antiques.

Stuart Kammerman

Stuart Kammerman, now retired, worked as a high school principal and school district superintendent. He is married and has two grown sons. A member of the international Paperweight Collectors Association, Inc., he has written articles about American glass advertising paperweights, both for that organization's annual bulletin and for the newsletter of the Antique Advertising Association of America. In addition to collecting and writing about antique American paperweights, Kammerman is also interested in collecting historical memorabilia from his hometown of Roseburg, Oregon. He is a lifelong and long-suffering fan of the Chicago Cubs.

COLLECTOR BOOKS

Informing Today's Collector

For over two decades we have been keeping collectors informed on trends and values in all fields of antiques and collectibles.

DOLLS, FIGURES & TEDDY BEARS

4707	A Decade of **Barbie Dolls** & Collectibles, 1981–1991, Summers	$19.95
4631	**Barbie Doll** Boom, 1986–1995, Augustyniak	$18.95
2079	**Barbie Doll** Fashion, Volume I, Eames	$24.95
4846	**Barbie Doll** Fashion, Volume II, Eames	$24.95
3957	**Barbie** Exclusives, Rana	$18.95
4632	**Barbie** Exclusives, Book II, Rana	$18.95
5672	The **Barbie Doll** Years, 4th Ed., Olds	$19.95
3810	**Chatty Cathy** Dolls, Lewis	$15.95
5352	Collector's Ency. of **Barbie** Doll Exclusives & More, 2nd Ed.,Augustyniak	$24.95
2211	Collector's Encyclopedia of **Madame Alexander** Dolls, Smith	$24.95
4863	Collector's Encyclopedia of **Vogue Dolls**, Izen/Stover	$29.95
5821	**Doll Values**, Antique to Modern, 5th Ed., Moyer	$12.95
5829	**Madame Alexander** Collector's Dolls Price Guide #26, Crowsey	$12.95
5833	**Modern Collectible Dolls**, Volume V, Moyer	$24.95
5689	**Nippon Dolls** & Playthings, Van Patten/Lau	$29.95
5365	**Peanuts Collectibles**, Podley/Bang	$24.95
5253	Story of **Barbie**, 2nd Ed., Westenhouser	$24.95
5277	**Talking Toys** of the 20th Century, Lewis	$15.95
1513	**Teddy Bears & Steiff** Animals, Mandel	$9.95
1817	**Teddy Bears & Steiff** Animals, 2nd Series, Mandel	$19.95
2084	**Teddy Bears, Annalee's & Steiff** Animals, 3rd Series, Mandel	$19.95
5371	**Teddy Bear** Treasury, Yenke	$19.95
1808	Wonder of **Barbie**, Manos	$9.95
1430	World of **Barbie** Dolls, Manos	$9.95
4880	World of **Raggedy Ann** Collectibles, Avery	$24.95

TOYS, MARBLES & CHRISTMAS COLLECTIBLES

2333	Antique & Collectible **Marbles**, 3rd Ed., Grist	$9.95
5353	**Breyer Animal** Collector's Guide, 2nd Ed., Browell	$19.95
4976	**Christmas Ornaments**, Lights & Decorations, Johnson	$24.95
4737	**Christmas Ornaments**, Lights & Decorations, Vol. II, Johnson	$24.95
4739	**Christmas Ornaments**, Lights & Decorations, Vol. III, Johnson	$24.95
4559	Collectible **Action Figures**, 2nd Ed., Manos	$17.95
2338	Collector's Encyclopedia of **Disneyana**, Longest, Stern	$24.95
5038	Collector's Guide to **Diecast Toys** & Scale Models, 2nd Ed., Johnson	$19.95
4651	Collector's Guide to **Tinker Toys**, Strange	$18.95
4566	Collector's Guide to **Tootsietoys**, 2nd Ed., Richter	$19.95
5169	Collector's Guide to **TV Toys** & Memorabilia, 2nd Ed., Davis/Morgan	$24.95
5360	**Fisher-Price Toys**, Cassity	$19.95
4720	The Golden Age of **Automotive Toys**, 1925–1941, Hutchison/Johnson	$24.95
5593	Grist's Big Book of **Marbles**, 2nd Ed.	$24.95
3970	Grist's Machine-Made & Contemporary **Marbles**, 2nd Ed.	$9.95
5267	**Matchbox Toys**, 1947 to 1998, 3rd Ed., Johnson	$19.95
5830	**McDonald's** Collectibles, 2nd Edition, Henriques/DuVall	$24.95
5673	Modern **Candy Containers** & Novelties, Brush/Miller	$19.95
1540	Modern **Toys** 1930–1980, Baker	$19.95
3888	**Motorcycle Toys**, Antique & Contemporary, Gentry/Downs	$18.95
5693	**Schroeder's Collectible Toys**, Antique to Modern Price Guide, 7th Ed.	$17.95

FURNITURE

1457	American **Oak** Furniture, McNerney	$9.95
3716	American **Oak** Furniture, Book II, McNerney	$12.95
1118	Antique **Oak** Furniture, Hill	$7.95
2271	Collector's Encyclopedia of **American** Furniture, Vol. II, Swedberg	$24.95
3720	Collector's Encyclopedia of **American** Furniture, Vol. III, Swedberg	$24.95
5359	Early **American** Furniture, Obbard	$12.95
1755	Furniture of the **Depression Era**, Swedberg	$19.95
3906	**Heywood-Wakefield** Modern Furniture, Rouland	$18.95
1885	**Victorian** Furniture, Our American Heritage, McNerney	$9.95
3829	**Victorian** Furniture, Our American Heritage, Book II, McNerney	$9.95

JEWELRY, HATPINS, WATCHES & PURSES

1712	Antique & Collectible **Thimbles** & Accessories, Mathis	$19.95
1748	Antique **Purses**, Revised Second Ed., Holiner	$19.95
1278	Art Nouveau & Art Deco **Jewelry**, Baker	$9.95
4850	Collectible **Costume Jewelry**, Simonds	$24.95
5675	Collectible **Silver Jewelry**, Rezazadeh	$24.95
3722	Collector's Ency. of **Compacts**, Carryalls & Face Powder Boxes, Mueller	$24.95
4940	**Costume Jewelry**, A Practical Handbook & Value Guide, Rezazadeh	$24.95
1716	Fifty Years of Collectible **Fashion Jewelry**, 1925–1975, Baker	$19.95
1424	**Hatpins** & Hatpin Holders, Baker	$9.95
5695	**Ladies' Vintage Accessories**, Bruton	$24.95
1181	100 Years of Collectible **Jewelry**, 1850–1950, Baker	$9.95
4729	**Sewing Tools** & Trinkets, Thompson	$24.95
5620	Unsigned Beauties of **Costume Jewelry**, Brown	$24.95
4878	Vintage & Contemporary **Purse Accessories**, Gerson	$24.95
5696	Vintage & Vogue Ladies' **Compacts**, 2nd Edition, Gerson	$29.95

INDIANS, GUNS, KNIVES, TOOLS, PRIMITIVES

1868	Antique **Tools**, Our American Heritage, McNerney	$9.95
5616	Big Book of **Pocket Knives**, Stewart	$19.95
4943	Field Guide to Flint **Arrowheads & Knives** of the North American Indian	$9.95
2279	**Indian Artifacts** of the Midwest, Book I, Hothem	$14.95
3885	**Indian Artifacts** of the Midwest, Book II, Hothem	$16.95
4870	**Indian Artifacts** of the Midwest, Book III, Hothem	$18.95
5685	**Indian Artifacts** of the Midwest, Book IV, Hothem	$19.95
5687	**Modern Guns**, Identification & Values, 13th Ed., Quertermous	$14.95
2164	**Primitives**, Our American Heritage, McNerney	$9.95
1759	**Primitives**, Our American Heritage, 2nd Series, McNerney	$14.95
4730	Standard **Knife** Collector's Guide, 3rd Ed., Ritchie & Stewart	$12.95

PAPER COLLECTIBLES & BOOKS

4633	**Big Little Books**, Jacobs	$18.95
4710	Collector's Guide to **Children's Books**, 1850 to 1950, Volume I, Jones	$18.95
5153	Collector's Guide to **Children's Books**, 1850 to 1950, Volume II, Jones	$19.95
5596	Collector's Guide to **Children's Books**, 1950 to 1975, Volume III, Jones	$19.95
1441	Collector's Guide to **Post Cards**, Wood	$9.95
2081	Guide to Collecting **Cookbooks**, Allen	$14.95
5825	Huxford's **Old Book** Value Guide, 13th Ed.	$19.95
2080	Price Guide to **Cookbooks** & Recipe Leaflets, Dickinson	$9.95
3973	**Sheet Music** Reference & Price Guide, 2nd Ed., Pafik & Guiheen	$19.95
4654	**Victorian Trade Cards**, Historical Reference & Value Guide, Cheadle	$19.95
4733	**Whitman Juvenile Books**, Brown	$17.95

GLASSWARE

5602	Anchor Hocking's **Fire-King** & More, 2nd Ed.	$24.95
4561	Collectible **Drinking Glasses**, Chase & Kelly	$17.95
5823	Collectible **Glass Shoes**, 2nd Edition, Wheatley	$24.95
5357	Coll. **Glassware** from the 40s, 50s & 60s, 5th Ed., Florence	$19.95
1810	Collector's Encyclopedia of **American Art Glass**, Shuman	$29.95
5358	Collector's Encyclopedia of **Depression Glass**, 14th Ed., Florence	$19.95
1961	Collector's Encyclopedia of **Fry Glassware**, Fry Glass Society	$24.95
1664	Collector's Encyclopedia of **Heisey Glass**, 1925–1938, Bredehoft	$24.95
3905	Collector's Encyclopedia of **Milk Glass**, Newbound	$24.95
4936	Collector's Guide to **Candy Containers**, Dezso/Poirier	$19.95
4564	**Crackle Glass**, Weitman	$19.95
4941	**Crackle Glass**, Book II, Weitman	$19.95
4714	**Czechoslovakian Glass** and Collectibles, Book II, Barta/Rose	$16.95
5528	Early American **Pattern Glass**, Metz	$17.95
5682	**Elegant Glassware** of the Depression Era, 9th Ed., Florence	$19.95
5614	Field Guide to **Pattern Glass**, McCain	$17.95
3981	Evers' Standard **Cut Glass** Value Guide	$12.95
4659	**Fenton** Art Glass, 1907–1939, Whitmyer	$24.95
5615	Florence's **Glassware Pattern Identification** Guide, Vol. II	$19.95

4719	**Fostoria**, Etched, Carved & Cut Designs, Vol. II, Kerr	$24.95
3883	**Fostoria Stemware**, The Crystal for America, Long/Seate	$24.95
5261	**Fostoria Tableware**, 1924 – 1943, Long/Seate	$24.95
5361	**Fostoria Tableware**, 1944 – 1986, Long/Seate	$24.95
5604	**Fostoria**, Useful & Ornamental, Long/Seate	$29.95
4644	**Imperial Carnival Glass**, Burns	$18.95
5827	**Kitchen Glassware** of the Depression Years, 6th Ed., Florence	$24.95
5600	Much More Early American **Pattern Glass**, Metz	$17.95
5690	Pocket Guide to **Depression Glass**, 12th Ed., Florence	$9.95
5594	Standard Encyclopedia of **Carnival Glass**, 7th Ed., Edwards/Carwile	$29.95
5595	Standard **Carnival Glass** Price Guide, 12th Ed., Edwards/Carwile	$9.95
5272	Standard Encyclopedia of **Opalescent Glass**, 3rd Ed., Edwards/Carwile	$24.95
5617	Standard Encyclopedia of **Pressed Glass**, 2nd Ed., Edwards/Carwile	$29.95
4731	**Stemware Identification**, Featuring Cordials with Values, Florence	$24.95
4732	**Very Rare Glassware** of the Depression Years, 5th Series, Florence	$24.95
4656	**Westmoreland Glass**, Wilson	$24.95

POTTERY

4927	**ABC Plates & Mugs**, Lindsay	$24.95
4929	**American Art Pottery**, Sigafoose	$24.95
4630	**American Limoges**, Limoges	$24.95
1312	**Blue & White Stoneware**, McNerney	$9.95
1958	So. Potteries **Blue Ridge Dinnerware**, 3rd Ed., Newbound	$14.95
1959	**Blue Willow**, 2nd Ed., Gaston	$14.95
4851	Collectible **Cups & Saucers**, Harran	$18.95
1373	Collector's Encyclopedia of **American Dinnerware**, Cunningham	$24.95
4931	Collector's Encyclopedia of **Bauer Pottery**, Chipman	$24.95
4932	Collector's Encyclopedia of **Blue Ridge Dinnerware**, Vol. II, Newbound	$24.95
4658	Collector's Encyclopedia of **Brush-McCoy Pottery**, Huxford	$24.95
5034	Collector's Encyclopedia of **California Pottery**, 2nd Ed., Chipman	$24.95
2133	Collector's Encyclopedia of **Cookie Jars**, Roerig	$24.95
3723	Collector's Encyclopedia of **Cookie Jars**, Book II, Roerig	$24.95
4939	Collector's Encyclopedia of **Cookie Jars**, Book III, Roerig	$24.95
5748	Collector's Encyclopedia of **Fiesta**, 9th Ed., Huxford	$24.95
4718	Collector's Encyclopedia of **Figural Planters & Vases**, Newbound	$19.95
3961	Collector's Encyclopedia of **Early Noritake**, Alden	$24.95
1439	Collector's Encyclopedia of **Flow Blue China**, Gaston	$19.95
3812	Collector's Encyclopedia of **Flow Blue China**, 2nd Ed., Gaston	$24.95
3431	Collector's Encyclopedia of **Homer Laughlin China**, Jasper	$24.95
1276	Collector's Encyclopedia of **Hull Pottery**, Roberts	$19.95
3962	Collector's Encyclopedia of **Lefton China**, DeLozier	$19.95
4855	Collector's Encyclopedia of **Lefton China**, Book II, DeLozier	$19.95
5609	Collector's Encyclopedia of **Limoges Porcelain**, 3rd Ed., Gaston	$29.95
2334	Collector's Encyclopedia of **Majolica Pottery**, Katz-Marks	$19.95
1358	Collector's Encyclopedia of **McCoy Pottery**, Huxford	$19.95
5677	Collector's Encyclopedia of **Niloak**, 2nd Edition, Gifford	$29.95
3837	Collector's Encyclopedia of **Nippon Porcelain**, Van Patten	$24.95
1665	Collector's Ency. of **Nippon Porcelain**, 3rd Series, Van Patten	$24.95
4712	Collector's Ency. of **Nippon Porcelain**, 4th Series, Van Patten	$24.95
5053	Collector's Ency. of **Nippon Porcelain**, 5th Series, Van Patten	$24.95
5678	Collector's Ency. of **Nippon Porcelain**, 6th Series, Van Patten	$29.95
1447	Collector's Encyclopedia of **Noritake**, Van Patten	$19.95
1038	Collector's Encyclopedia of **Occupied Japan**, 2nd Series, Florence	$14.95
4951	Collector's Encyclopedia of **Old Ivory China**, Hillman	$24.95
5564	Collector's Encyclopedia of **Pickard China**, Reed	$29.95
3877	Collector's Encyclopedia of **R.S. Prussia**, 4th Series, Gaston	$24.95
5679	Collector's Encyclopedia of **Red Wing Art Pottery**, Dollen	$24.95
5618	Collector's Encyclopedia of **Rosemeade Pottery**, Dommel	$24.95
5841	Collector's Encyclopedia of **Roseville Pottery**, Revised, Huxford/Nickel	$24.95
5842	Collector's Encyclopedia of **Roseville Pottery**, 2nd Series, Huxford/Nickel	$24.95
4713	Collector's Encyclopedia of **Salt Glaze Stoneware**, Taylor/Lowrance	$24.95
3314	Collector's Encyclopedia of **Van Briggle Art Pottery**, Sasicki	$24.95
4563	Collector's Encyclopedia of **Wall Pockets**, Newbound	$19.95
2111	Collector's Encyclopedia of **Weller Pottery**, Huxford	$29.95
5680	Collector's Guide to **Feather Edge Ware**, McAllister	$19.95
3876	Collector's Guide to **Lu-Ray Pastels**, Meehan	$18.95

3814	Collector's Guide to **Made in Japan Ceramics**, White	$18.95
4646	Collector's Guide to **Made in Japan Ceramics**, Book II, White	$18.95
2339	Collector's Guide to **Shawnee Pottery**, Vanderbilt	$19.95
1425	**Cookie Jars**, Westfall	$9.95
3440	**Cookie Jars**, Book II, Westfall	$19.95
4924	Figural & Novelty **Salt & Pepper Shakers**, 2nd Series, Davern	$24.95
2379	Lehner's Ency. of **U.S. Marks** on Pottery, Porcelain & China	$24.95
4722	**McCoy Pottery**, Collector's Reference & Value Guide, Hanson/Nissen	$19.95
5691	**Post86 Fiesta**, Identification & Value Guide, Racheter	$19.95
1670	**Red Wing Collectibles**, DePasquale	$9.95
1440	**Red Wing Stoneware**, DePasquale	$9.95
1632	**Salt & Pepper Shakers**, Guarnaccia	$9.95
5091	**Salt & Pepper Shakers** II, Guarnaccia	$18.95
3443	**Salt & Pepper Shakers** IV, Guarnaccia	$18.95
3738	**Shawnee Pottery**, Mangus	$24.95
4629	Turn of the Century **American Dinnerware**, 1880s–1920s, Jasper	$24.95
3327	**Watt Pottery** – Identification & Value Guide, Morris	$19.95

OTHER COLLECTIBLES

5838	Advertising **Thermometers**, Merritt	$16.95
4704	Antique & Collectible **Buttons**, Wisniewski	$19.95
2269	Antique **Brass & Copper** Collectibles, Gaston	$16.95
1880	Antique **Iron**, McNerney	$9.95
3872	Antique **Tins**, Dodge	$24.95
4845	Antique **Typewriters & Office Collectibles**, Rehr	$19.95
5607	Antiquing and Collecting on the **Internet**, Parry	$12.95
1128	**Bottle** Pricing Guide, 3rd Ed., Cleveland	$7.95
3718	Collectible **Aluminum**, Grist	$16.95
4560	Collectible **Cats**, An Identification & Value Guide, Book II, Fyke	$19.95
5060	Collectible **Souvenir Spoons**, Bednersh	$19.95
5676	Collectible **Souvenir Spoons**, Book II, Bednersh	$29.95
5666	Collector's Encyclopedia of **Granite Ware**, Book 2, Greguire	$29.95
5836	Collector's Guide to **Antique Radios**, 5th Ed., Bunis	$19.95
5608	Collector's Gde. to Buying, Selling & Trading on the **Internet**, 2nd Ed., Hix	$12.95
4637	Collector's Guide to **Cigarette Lighters**, Book II, Flanagan	$17.95
3966	Collector's Guide to **Inkwells**, Identification & Values, Badders	$18.95
4947	Collector's Guide to **Inkwells**, Book II, Badders	$19.95
5681	Collector's Guide to **Lunchboxes**, White	$19.95
5621	Collector's Guide to **Online Auctions**, Hix	$12.95
4862	Collector's Guide to **Toasters** & Accessories, Greguire	$19.95
4652	Collector's Guide to **Transistor Radios**, 2nd Ed., Bunis	$16.95
4864	Collector's Guide to **Wallace Nutting Pictures**, Ivankovich	$18.95
1629	**Doorstops**, Identification & Values, Bertoia	$9.95
5683	**Fishing Lure** Collectibles, 2nd Ed., Murphy/Edmisten	$29.95
5259	**Flea Market Trader**, 12th Ed., Huxford	$9.95
4945	**G-Men and FBI Toys** and Collectibles, Whitworth	$18.95
5605	**Garage Sale & Flea Market Annual**, 8th Ed.	$19.95
3819	**General Store** Collectibles, Wilson	$24.95
5159	Huxford's Collectible **Advertising**, 4th Ed.	$24.95
2216	**Kitchen Antiques**, 1790–1940, McNerney	$14.95
5686	**Lighting Fixtures** of the Depression Era, Book I, Thomas	$24.95
4950	The **Lone Ranger**, Collector's Reference & Value Guide, Felbinger	$18.95
2026	**Railroad** Collectibles, 4th Ed., Baker	$14.95
5619	**Roy Rogers and Dale Evans** Toys & Memorabilia, Coyle	$24.95
5692	**Schroeder's Antiques Price Guide**, 19th Ed., Huxford	$14.95
5007	**Silverplated Flatware**, Revised 4th Edition, Hagan	$18.95
5694	Summers' Guide to **Coca-Cola**, 3rd Ed.	$24.95
5356	Summers' Pocket Guide to **Coca-Cola**, 2nd Ed.	$9.95
3892	**Toy & Miniature Sewing Machines**, Thomas	$18.95
4876	**Toy & Miniature Sewing Machines**, Book II, Thomas	$24.95
5144	Value Guide to **Advertising Memorabilia**, 2nd Ed., Summers	$19.95
3977	Value Guide to **Gas Station Memorabilia**, Summers & Priddy	$24.95
4877	Vintage **Bar Ware**, Visakay	$24.95
4935	The W.F. Cody **Buffalo Bill** Collector's Guide with Values	$24.95
5281	**Wanted to Buy**, 7th Edition	$9.95

This is only a partial listing of the books on antiques that are available from Collector Books. All books are well illustrated and contain current values. Most of these books are available from your local bookseller, antique dealer, or public library. If you are unable to locate certain titles in your area, you may order by mail from COLLECTOR BOOKS, P.O. Box 3009, Paducah, KY 42002-3009. Customers with Visa, Discover or MasterCard may phone in orders from 7:00–5:00 CST, Monday–Friday, Toll Free 1-800-626-5420, or online at www.collectorbooks.com. Add $3.00 for postage for the first book ordered and 50¢ for each additional book. Include item number, title, and price when ordering. Allow 14 to 21 days for delivery.

Schroeder's ANTIQUES Price Guide

OUR #1 BEST-SELLER!

...is the #1 bestselling antiques & collectibles value guide on the market today, and here's why...

- *More than 450 advisors, well-known dealers, and top-notch collectors work together with our editors to bring you accurate information regarding pricing and identification.*

- *More than 50,000 items in over 600 categories are listed along with hundreds of sharp original photos that illustrate not only the rare and unusual, but the common, popular collectibles as well.*

- *Each large close-up shot shows important details clearly. Every subject is represented with histories and background information, a feature not found in any of our competitors' publications.*

- *Our editors keep abreast of newly developing trends, often adding several new categories a year as the need arises.*

Schroeder's
ANTIQUES
Price Guide

OUR #1 BEST-SELLER!

Identification & Values of Over 50,000 Antiques & Collectibles

8½" x 11"
608 pages
$14.95

If it merits the interest of today's collector, you'll find it in *Schroeder's*. And you can feel confident that the information we publish is up-to-date and accurate. Our advisors thoroughly check each category to spot inconsistencies, listings that may not be entirely reflective of market dealings, and lines too vague to be of merit. Only the best of the lot remains for publication.

Without doubt, you'll find
Schroeder's Antiques Price Guide
the only one to buy for reliable information and values.

cb

COLLECTOR BOOKS
P.O. Box 3009 • Paducah, KY 42002–3009
www.collectorbooks.com